HOW TO DESIGN QUESTIONS AND TASKS TO ASSESS STUDENT THINKING

HOW TO DESIGN QUESTIONS AND TASKS TO ASSESS STUDENT THINKING

SUSAN M. BROOKHART

ASCD | Alexandria, Virginia USA

ASCD

1703 N. Beauregard St. • Alexandria, VA 22311-1714 USA
Phone: 800-933-2723 or 703-578-9600 • Fax: 703-575-5400
Website: www.ascd.org • E-mail: member@ascd.org
Author guidelines: www.ascd.org/write

Judy Seltz, *Acting Executive Director;* Richard Papale, *Acting Chief Program Development Officer;* Stefani Roth, *Interim Publisher;* Genny Ostertag, *Acquisitions Editor;* Julie Houtz, *Director, Book Editing & Production;* Miriam Goldstein, *Editor;* Sima Nasr, *Senior Graphic Designer;* Mike Kalyan, *Manager, Production Services;* Valerie Younkin, *Production Designer*

PAPERBACK ISBN: 978-1-4166-1924-6 ASCD product #114014

ASCD Member Book No. FY14-9 (Aug 2014 P). ASCD Member Books mail to Premium (P), Select (S), and Institutional Plus (I+) members on this schedule: Jan, PSI+; Feb, P; Apr, PSI+; May, P; Jul, PSI+; Aug, P; Sep, PSI+; Nov, PSI+; Dec, P. For current details on membership, see www.ascd.org/membership and www.ascd.org/memberbooks.

Also available as an e-book (see Books in Print for the ISBNs).

Quantity discounts: 10–49, 10%; 50+, 15%; 1,000+, special discounts (e-mail programteam@ascd.org or call 800-933-2723, ext. 5773, or 703-575-5773). Also available in e-book formats. For desk copies, go to www.ascd.org/deskcopy.

Library of Congress Cataloging-in-Publication Data
Brookhart, Susan M.
How to design questions and tasks to assess student thinking / Susan M. Brookhart.
pages cm
Includes bibliographical references and index.
ISBN 978-1-4166-1924-6 (pbk. : alk. paper) 1. Educational tests and measurements—United States. 2. Educational evaluation—United States. 3. Thought and thinking—Study and teaching—United States. 4. Critical thinking—Study and teaching—United States. I. Title.
LB3051.B7286 2014
371.26—dc23

2014016246

23 22 21 20 19 18 17 16 15 14 1 2 3 4 5 6 7 8 9 10 11 12 13

This book is dedicated to all the teachers,
administrators, and other educators who
work so tirelessly to help students learn to think.
I am indebted to the teachers who did that for me
and inspired by those who do so now. It is not too
dramatic to say the future is in their hands.

HOW TO DESIGN

QUESTIONS AND TASKS

TO ASSESS STUDENT THINKING

1 | Assessing Higher-Order Thinking: Five *W*s and an *H*

In Liam's 5th grade science class, students memorize the properties of solids, liquids, and gases. They take quizzes with questions such as "The temperature at which a solid changes to a liquid is called the ____________." They answer questions such as "What happens when water boils?" by finding the appropriate explanations in their textbook and rewriting them in their own words to show they understand.

Fifth grader Olivia's science class uses the same textbook. The students take some quizzes, too. Most of their questions, however, are more like this: "Water boils at a lower temperature in the mountains than it does at sea level. Sam lives in the mountains. He is boiling carrots to serve at dinner. Would it take a longer or shorter time to cook the carrots than it would take at sea level? Explain your answer."

Both of these 5th graders are learning about states of matter. But Olivia will learn more and remember it longer than Liam. The kinds of questions her teacher asks help her use her knowledge of states of matter, connecting it to other knowledge and reasoning processes, and at the same time show her that there is a purpose for knowing these things.

WHO Is Likely to Benefit from Assessment of Higher-Order Thinking?

The Liams and Olivias of the world are the future, and they will need to learn to think. The world is changing quickly, and students will need to develop higher-order thinking skills and use them throughout their lives. If you don't already believe that students will truly benefit from assessment of higher-order thinking, I hope this chapter convinces you. If you do already believe it, this chapter will give you some important foundational ideas, in the form of five *W*s (including this first one, "who") and an *H*.

WHAT Does Assessment of Higher-Order Thinking Look Like?

Alexander and her colleagues (2011) propose a definition of higher-order thinking that will serve well for this book:

> Higher-order thinking is the mental engagement with ideas, objects, and situations in an analogical, elaborative, inductive, deductive, and otherwise transformational manner that is indicative of an orientation toward knowing as a complex, effortful, generative, evidence-seeking, and reflective enterprise. (p. 53)

Two big ideas stand out in this definition. One, higher-order thinking happens when students engage with what they know in such a way as to *transform* it. That is, this kind of thinking doesn't just reproduce the same knowledge; it results in something new. A student who analyzes a poem, for example, doesn't just recite the poem or copy it into her notebook. She identifies literary elements and techniques used in the poem and creates an interpretation based on those elements and techniques. The poem as a whole is transformed into parts and then re-formed into an interpretation. Something new is created. Important for this book is the point that the teacher would look at that creation as evidence of the thinking that went on inside the student's head.

The second big idea in this definition is the conception of knowledge as an enterprise that is "complex, effortful, generative, evidence-seeking, and reflective."

Higher-order thinking only makes sense if to truly "know" something means that you can use it and transform it. In my 2010 book *How to Assess Higher-Order Thinking Skills in Your Classroom*, I summarized three ways in which teachers have conventionally thought about how students use knowledge: transfer, critical thinking, and problem solving. These three ways of thinking about using knowledge are not mutually exclusive. They all have in common that students apply what they know to an idea, an object, or a situation—as the definition says—and transform it into something new.

Higher-order thinking is often associated with the work of Bloom, Engelhart, Furst, Hill, and Krathwohl (1956). In fact, Bloom and his colleagues tried to avoid the idea that analysis, synthesis, and evaluation were somehow "above" knowledge, comprehension, and application in a hierarchical sense. However, the idea of helping students develop skills at using the knowledge they gain remains a value for educators, and turning to Bloom's or some other taxonomy is a common and practical way to do that. In this book, I refer to "Bloom's taxonomy" mostly in terms of the cognitive-process dimension of the revised Bloom's taxonomy (Anderson & Krathwohl, 2001): Remember, Understand, Apply, Analyze, Evaluate, Create.

Both tests and performance assessments can tap higher-order thinking. In this book, I use the word *test* to mean a paper-and-pencil or computer-based set of questions that students must answer, typically in a relatively short, fixed time period and in a supervised setting. The questions that are on tests are sometimes called *test items*, but in this book I mostly just call them *questions*.

A *performance assessment* has two parts: a task for students to perform and a scoring scheme to judge the performance. Performance assessment tasks can require students to demonstrate a process (e.g., sing a song, recite a Shakespeare monologue, use safety equipment properly) or produce a product (e.g., a report, a diorama, a sculpture). What the performance assessment asks students to do is called the *task*. This book is mostly concerned with writing performance tasks, not scoring schemes, although a performance assessment is not complete without both. In discussing performance tasks, I necessarily talk about what to look for in the work and how the task should connect with a scoring scheme. More comprehensive information about rubrics and other scoring schemes appears in *How to Create and Use Rubrics for Formative Assessment and Grading* (Brookhart, 2013b).

WHEN Should I Assess Higher-Order Thinking?

The short answer to this question is "Always." In this book, I take the point of view that you should (almost) always assess higher-order thinking. Of course, you begin planning for instruction and assessment with your state standards and your curriculum's instructional goals and objectives. Most of the time, these will include some expectations for higher-order thinking. In the few instances when they don't (for example, if the goal is memorizing a multiplication table), I advocate adding opportunities for students to make connections between what you are teaching and other things they know or with their own experience.

WHERE in My Instruction Should I Plan to Assess Higher-Order Thinking?

Assess higher-order thinking during all parts of instruction and assessment, both formative and summative. You can use higher-order thinking *questions* in many instances—oral class discussion, quizzes, exit tickets and other classroom strategies, and tests. You can use higher-order thinking *tasks* in many instances as well—classroom learning activities, performance assessments, and short- and long-term projects. The most important point here is that higher-order thinking questions and tasks should be infused throughout instruction and assessment. Don't wait until students have memorized some facts and then ask them to reason with the facts as a second step. Thinking should begin from the minute you share your learning target with students.

WHY Should I Assess Higher-Order Thinking?

There are lots of reasons to assess higher-order thinking in your classroom. Here are four of them:

- What you assess is a signal to students about what you think is important to learn.
- What you assess helps define what students will, in fact, learn.
- Assessing higher-order thinking skills leads to improved student learning and motivation.

- The Common Core State Standards and other next-generation standards require teaching and assessing higher-order thinking.

I'd like to say a little more about those last two reasons.

Thinking and Learning

Research suggests that students who are asked to think learn better. Higgins, Hall, Baumfield, and Moseley (2005) reviewed research studies that looked at the effects of thinking-skills interventions on student cognition, achievement, and attitudes. They used the method of meta-analysis, reporting effect sizes (the amount of change in standard deviation units) for the studies. For the purposes of their review, Higgins and colleagues defined *thinking-skills interventions* as "approaches or programmes which identify for learners translatable mental processes and/or which require learners to plan, describe, and evaluate their thinking and learning" (p. 7).

The researchers found 29 studies, mostly from the United States and the United Kingdom, that were appropriate for their investigation. These studies were conducted in primary (9) and secondary (20) schools, and most were in the curriculum areas of literacy (7), mathematics (9), and science (9). The researchers found that the average effect sizes of thinking-skills instruction were as follows:

- 0.62 on cognitive outcomes (for example, verbal and nonverbal reasoning tests), over 29 studies.
- 0.62 on achievement of curricular outcomes (for example, reading, math, or science tests), over 19 studies.
- 1.44 on affective outcomes (attitudes and motivation), over 6 studies.

Because of the small number of effect sizes of affective outcomes, the average effect-size estimate of 1.44 may be less reliable than the other two effect sizes, which are drawn from a larger number of studies. And although an effect size of 0.62 may seem small in comparison to 1.44, even 0.62 is a large effect for an educational intervention.

Abrami and his colleagues (2008) did a meta-analysis of thinking-skills interventions on measures of critical thinking itself. Although critical thinking is not exactly the same thing as higher-order thinking as defined here, there is much overlap; critical-thinking skills include "interpretation, analysis, evaluation, inference, explanation, and self-regulation" (p. 1103). Abrami and his colleagues found 117 studies with participants ranging from elementary school students through adults. The average effect size of thinking-skills interventions on developing thinking skills was 0.34 over all the effects in all the studies. However, average effects on the thinking skills of elementary students (6- through 10-year-olds, 0.52) and secondary students (11- through 15-year-olds, 0.69) were higher than were those for undergraduate college students (0.25).

Taken together, these two meta-analyses suggest that teaching thinking skills to elementary and secondary students affects the development of those same thinking skills, achievement in school subjects, and motivation, all at about the same level. The effect size of 0.62 that Higgins and his colleagues found for achievement in school subjects is equivalent to moving an "average" class of students from the 50th percentile to the 73rd percentile on a standardized measure, such as a reading or math test.

Standards

The Common Core and other standards require higher-order thinking. The standards-based reform movement actually began in the 1980s as a reaction to the "minimum competency" movement in the 1970s that had emphasized basic skills. Educators and the public quickly discovered that "the minimum became the maximum," and that minimum-competency testing on basic skills was actually de-skilling students (Brookhart, 2013c). In the 1980s, states and professional organizations began working on standards that included higher-order thinking. Parallel developments occurred in performance assessment, requiring students to use knowledge instead of simply recalling it.

At this point, because of the Common Core State Standards (www.corestandards.org), the Next Generation Science Standards (www.nextgenscience.org), and the Framework for Social Studies State Standards (www.socialstudies.org/c3), it is possible to describe some of the specific thinking skills that are or will be required for most students in the United States. But a cursory treatment here will not do the standards justice. Make sure to investigate standards in the areas you teach, probing in much greater detail than what I include here. Nevertheless, the lists that follow do show that the thinking skills required in current standards for student achievement match the two big ideas in the definition of higher-order thinking—namely, that higher-order thinking happens when students engage with what they know in such a way as to *transform* it, and that real knowledge is complex, effortful, generative, evidence-seeking, and reflective.

The Common Core State Standards for English Language Arts & Literacy in History/Social Studies, Science, and Technical Subjects (National Governors Association Center for Best Practices [NGA Center] & Council of Chief State School Officers [CCSSO], 2010a) organizes standards as progressions across grades within anchor standards. For reading (both literature and informational text), those anchor standards are as follows:

- Key ideas and details.
- Craft and structure [of the text].
- Integration of knowledge and ideas.
- Range of reading and level of text complexity.

For writing, the anchor standards are as follows:

- Text types and purposes.
- Production and distribution of writing.
- Research to build and present knowledge.
- Range of writing.

You can see from the wording of the anchor standards that the emphasis is on purpose-driven understanding of what a student reads or writes. A key underlying concept is the relationship among the text, other "texts" (both written texts and other knowledge and experiences), and oneself (the reader or writer). All of these pass our two-pronged test of "higher-order" thinking: using knowledge to transform, and in the process, seeking evidence, reflecting, and generating new knowledge.

The Common Core State Standards for Mathematics (NGA Center & CCSSO, 2010b) lists two kinds of standards: content standards and mathematical practice standards. Although thinking is an integral part of the content standards themselves, the mathematical practice standards, like the reading standards, are an explicit and intentional list of the kinds of mathematical thinking that students should learn how to do. There are eight mathematical practice standards that cut across grade levels:

- Make sense of problems and persevere in solving them.
- Reason abstractly and quantitatively.
- Construct viable arguments and critique the reasoning of others.
- Model with mathematics.
- Use appropriate tools strategically.
- Attend to precision.
- Look for and make use of structure.
- Look for and express regularity in repeated reasoning.

Once again, the twin themes of using knowledge to transform, and in the process, seeking evidence, reflecting, and generating new knowledge, are in evidence.

The Next Generation Science Standards are based on the National Research Council (NRC)'s *Framework for K–12 Science Education* (2012). Like the Common Core State Standards for Mathematics, the science standards contain an explicit and intentional list of the kinds of scientific thinking that students should learn how to do. They are called "science and engineering practices," and their goal is to "cultivate students' scientific habits of mind, develop their capability to engage in scientific inquiry, and teach them how to reason in a scientific context" (p. 41). The NRC notes that the field of science has had a historical tension between a narrow focus on teaching scientific facts, which leads to a naïve and incomplete understanding of science, and teaching scientific inquiry and reasoning. Wisely, the NRC opted for both. Actually, the framework has three major foci: science and engineering practices, crosscutting concepts, and disciplinary core ideas. Although higher-order thinking is an integral part of all three, the science and engineering practices make it particularly clear that the science standards require higher-order thinking. Here are the eight practices:

- Asking questions (for science) and defining problems (for engineering).
- Developing and using models.

- Planning and carrying out investigations.
- Analyzing and interpreting data.
- Using mathematics and computational thinking.
- Constructing explanations (for science) and designing solutions (for engineering).
- Engaging in argument from evidence.
- Obtaining, evaluating, and communicating information.

Yet again, the twin themes of using knowledge to transform, and in the process seeking evidence, reflecting, and generating new knowledge, are in evidence in the science standards as they were for mathematics and English language arts.

The College, Career, and Civic Life (C3) Framework for Social Studies State Standards (National Council for the Social Studies [NCSS], 2013) was developed by representatives from state education agencies, with input from the NCSS and other professional groups, to guide states in enhancing the rigor of K–12 civics, economics, geography, and history. The goal is to prepare students not only for college and career but also for informed civic life: "Now more than ever, students need the intellectual power to recognize societal problems; ask good questions and develop robust investigations into them; consider possible solutions and consequences; separate evidence-based claims from parochial opinions; and communicate and act upon what they learn" (p. 6). The C3 Framework is organized into four dimensions:

- Developing questions and planning inquiries.
- Applying disciplinary concepts and tools.
- Evaluating sources.
- Communicating conclusions and taking informed action.

Once again, students are called upon to use knowledge to transform, and in the process, to seek evidence, reflect, and generate new knowledge.

The thinking skills required by the standards for these core disciplines are impressive. Listing them one after another as I just did renders the message loud and clear: students are going to be expected to learn to think. Research suggests this will make them even better thinkers. Teachers, therefore, need to understand how to write the questions and tasks that will elicit higher-order thinking from their students. Such questions and tasks need to become a daily occurrence in next-generation classrooms.

HOW Can I Assess Higher-Order Thinking?

The rest of this book explains how to actually write questions and tasks that assess higher-order thinking. Chapter 2 offers a view of assessment questions and tasks as problems to solve. This view helps ensure that the questions and tasks you pose for students do, in fact, require the transforming of knowledge that our definition of higher-order thinking requires. Chapter 3 describes the range of assessment options that you can use to assess higher-order thinking. Both test questions and performance assessment tasks can be used in this way. Most of the remaining chapters show how to write different kinds of questions and tasks to assess higher-order thinking: multiple-choice questions, open-ended questions, and performance assessment tasks that focus on skills or processes, products, or long-term projects. A final chapter discusses some management issues in the assessment of higher-order thinking. Two appendices offer directions on using a test blueprint to plan a test and using a protocol to review assessment tasks.

2 Assessment Questions and Tasks as "Problems to Solve"

Our dog Lizzie is really smart, for a dog. She understands many words, knows lots of household and play routines, has a great sense of direction, and can figure out how to open almost any kind of latch that doesn't require using opposable thumbs. But she does not solve problems using higher-order thinking. For example, she has a morning routine that involves getting a treat, going outside to potty, and eating breakfast. If you tell her, "Go eat your breakfast," she perks right up and goes to the laundry room, where the food bowl is. If you tell her, "Go potty," she trots right to the back door and waits to be let out. But if you ask her, "Do you want to go potty or eat breakfast first?" she looks at you with big brown eyes and no understanding. The idea of prioritizing, or even of thinking about two things in relation to one another, is not part of her repertoire.

Contrast this with what a child can do. Even young children could answer the question about breakfast or potty. Most of them could tell you why they picked the answer they did; they could cite a reason relevant to the question (e.g., "I'm hungry"). Higher-order thinking is a part of human life, and with a little design work, it can and should become a bigger part of learning than it currently is in many schools.

Taking the Perspective of "Student as Problem Solver"

Problem solving is a great metaphor for most higher-order thinking tasks and for most assessment tasks that tap higher-order thinking. From simple decision making (Breakfast or bathroom first?) to interpretation of complex text (What did the white whale symbolize in *Moby-Dick*?) to planning and carrying out inquiry (What would happen to the atmosphere if greenhouse gas emissions were reduced by half?), students have to figure out the answer to the question "What am I being asked to do?" Then, they have to figure out what tools and strategies they have that would help them do whatever it is. Next, they have to select one or more tools or strategies and implement them. Finally, they have to review the result and decide whether they have indeed accomplished what they had been asked to do. This sounds just like classic descriptions of problem solving (Bransford & Stein, 1984).

In this book, thinking about assessment questions and tasks as problems for students to solve is a way to help identify what exactly a given question or task is assessing. From the student's point of view, when presented with a question or task, the first order of business is to identify "What is this question really asking me to do?" An important point is that the answer to this question should exactly match the knowledge or skill that the question or task is intended to assess. This is sometimes called *alignment*, and it's a very big deal. If the question or task elicits from the student something other than what is intended, then the assessment results won't mean what you think they mean. This is why the first order of business when designing and writing questions and tasks is to identify what learning outcome you need to assess.

I invite you to use the strategy of thinking through questions and tasks you write from the students' point of view as they "solve the problem" in order to identify what content and thinking skills the question or task calls up. Using the lens of a student solving the problem presented by the question or task makes it easier to identify questions or tasks according to any of the categories teachers may use (or, sometimes, have to use): Bloom's taxonomy, Webb's Depth of Knowledge levels, the Common Core Standards for Mathematical Practice, Science and Engineering Practices, and so on.

Examples in Math and Science

Let's walk through a couple of examples of simple performance tasks to demonstrate how useful this process can be for understanding just what an assessment task is able to show about what students know and can do. Let's start with the following math task.

On the grid below, plot the points with coordinates (B, 1), (B, 3), and (B, 4).

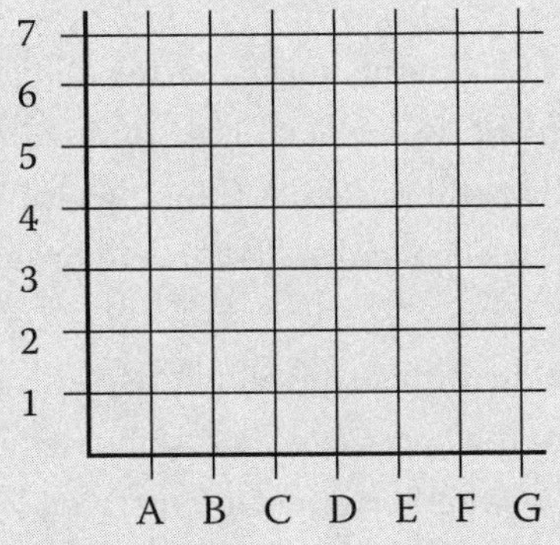

Plot three more points on the grid so that when you connect all six points you will have a rectangle. List the coordinates for the three new points. _____ _____ _____

Connect the six points to show your rectangle. Explain how you decided where to put your three points. ______________________________

Source: National Assessment of Educational Progress (NAEP) released items: 2009, grade 4, block M10, question #16. Adapted to allow for more than one correct answer.

Approaching this mathematics performance assessment from the student's point of view, we might come up with something like this: *What is this problem asking me to do? First, I must plot points. That means I must know what ordered pairs are and how to plot them on a grid. Then, I must decide on three more points that, with the three I already have, will make a rectangle, plot them, and connect them. Therefore, I must also know what a rectangle is and how to decide whether I have made one. Finally, I must explain my reasoning, which means I must be able to communicate my mathematical ideas in words as well as points on a grid.*

Summarizing the reasoning that teachers use to evaluate assessments, we can identify what content knowledge and skills and what thinking skills this question taps:

- Content Knowledge—Understand ordered pairs, grids, and rectangles.
- Content Skills—Plot points on a grid, connect points with a line.
- Thinking Skills—Create an original rectangle to satisfy given conditions, analyze one's own thinking about how to solve the problem, communicate mathematical reasoning in words.

Create and Analyze are, in Bloom's taxonomy terms, forms of higher-order thinking. Communicating original thinking is a special case of creating, in which the student needs to craft sentences that will make her thinking visible to a reader.

Aha! That's quite a list of knowledge and skills for one problem, even if that problem is a performance assessment.

Listing the knowledge and skills in this way allows us, with our teacher hats back on, to ask whether these were the knowledge and skills we intended to assess or not. If we just wanted to know whether our students could plot points, this assessment does not match our intentions. But if we wanted to know whether our students could use what they know about plotting points to solve a problem and reason mathematically, then this assessment does match our intentions.

I hope this demonstration illustrates how what students actually do when approaching a question or task is the key to defining what the question or task assesses. Now let's try the process on another performance task, this time in science.

> At your lab stations, you will find seven unknown solutions labeled *A* through *G*. You will also need pH paper, a pH scale, and paper or a computer for recording your observations and writing your conclusions. Dip a piece of pH paper into each solution and compare the color of the pH paper with the pH scale. Make a chart with two columns, one for each solution's name (*A*–*G*) and one for its pH value. Make a second chart placing the solutions in order from the most acidic to the most basic. Write a paragraph describing what you did and what you found. Which of the solutions were acids, and which were bases?

Again, let's look at this task from the student's point of view: *What problem am I being asked to solve? What is this task asking me to do? First, I must decide if I have all the materials I will need. I can do that by checking to make sure that what is at my lab station matches the list. Next, I need to dip a piece of pH paper into a solution, compare its color with the pH scale, and read off the appropriate number. I need to know how to distinguish acids (pH < 7) from bases (pH > 7). Next, I need to follow directions to make a two-column chart, and then be able to order numbers from low to high. Finally, I need to be able to recount what I did—which should match what the directions told me to do.*

Now, putting our teacher hats back on, we are able to analyze the content knowledge and skills and the thinking skills that are required for this task. Despite the hands-on nature of the task, which might lead you to think that higher-order thinking is involved, the student does not need to move beyond the Apply level of thinking, in Bloom's taxonomy terms. Translating the student reasoning in the previous paragraph to the language that teachers use to evaluate assessments, we can identify what content knowledge and skills and what thinking skills this question taps:

- Content Knowledge—Know the words *pH, acid, base*; identify pH paper and a pH scale; know pH scale divides between acids and bases at 7.
- Content Skills—Use pH paper, record data in a chart, order numbers from lowest to highest.
- Thinking Skills—Apply rule for classifying acids and bases, recount how directions were followed.

Apply, in Bloom's taxonomy terms, means employing a rule or procedure to a situation to arrive at a correct answer.

I hope this exercise in analyzing two assessment tasks as "problems to solve" from a student's point of view helps you see that neither the topic of the assessment nor the amount of hands-on activity is sufficient to determine whether the task actually requires students to engage in higher-order thinking. The first task looked like a rather conventional math problem but in fact was an open-ended performance assessment that required original thinking based on students' understanding of a coordinate plane. Not all the good answers would look alike. The second task seemed to be a fun experiment but in fact was a closed-ended task that required mostly following directions. All the good answers would look the same. In fact, there wasn't anything in the science task that required students to understand pH as anything more than a measurement scale for acids and bases. They didn't need to have a deep understanding of what the pH scale meant (a measure of hydrogen ion activity) and why it measured degree of acidity. All they needed to do to be successful was to be able to carry out the measurement procedure (dip, compare color with scale, read off a number, and record it).

* * * * * *

In Chapters 4 through 8, we'll take a look at how to craft assessments with deliberate attention to how to ensure that the questions or tasks require students to use higher-order thinking, to make their thinking visible and available for appraisal in some way, and to receive feedback (or, ultimately, a grade) on the quality of their thinking as well as their content knowledge and skills. First, though, Chapter 3 will describe the "assessment toolkit"—that is, the complete set of assessment methods from which we will select those with special affinity for assessing higher-order thinking in Chapters 4 through 8.

As you look at all the examples, use the student-perspective strategy detailed in this chapter—*What problem am I solving? What is the question asking me to do?* Don't take my word for what a question or task assesses: demonstrate it for yourself. In other words, as a reader, engage in some higher-order thinking of your own. I include in Appendix B a protocol you will find useful if you want to analyze tasks with colleagues at your school.

3 The Assessment Toolkit

Selecting the right tool for the job is important. If you need to pound a nail, select a hammer. I sometimes find that a major limitation of my already minimal handyperson skills is simply not knowing what tool is required to do a job—much less whether or not we have one in our garage or basement.

This chapter describes the assessment "tools" that are available for different assessment purposes. The array of assessment possibilities is actually quite broad—much broader than the assessments in many teachers' past experiences. Knowing what all the possibilities are will allow you to review your options and select the best tool for your purpose and context. Only when you have selected an assessment option with the potential to give you the information you seek, whether it's about higher-order thinking or anything else, will the "how-to-write-it" advice in Chapters 4 through 8 help you.

There are many ways to sort the assessment options available to you. One way is to use the degree of "construction" students need to do to respond. Bennett (1993) uses a taxonomy to express the continuum of how much construction is required by various assessment types. His list, presented in order from least to most amount of construction required, is multiple choice, selection/identification, reordering/rearrangement, substitution/correction, completion, construction, and presentation (pp. 3–4). Snow (1993) uses a slightly different taxonomy to express the continuum of the amount of student construction required by different assessment types. In order of amount of construction, he lists multiple choice, multiple choice with intervening construction, simple completion/cloze procedure, short-answer essay/complex completion, problem exercise, teach-back procedure (explaining a concept, procedure, structure, or system), long essay/demonstration project, and collections of above over time (e.g., a portfolio) (p. 48).

Another way to sort the assessment options available to you is to enumerate types of assessments that are different in terms of classroom practice. In such a list, the different methods do not form a continuum of the amount of student construction a response requires; rather, they are described in terms of their differences in how they would play out for students and teachers in a classroom. The role of students and teachers is different when students are taking a test, writing an essay, performing something, and answering questions.

Stiggins and his colleagues have created two versions of this type of taxonomy of classroom assessments. Stiggins (1992) developed a two-dimensional taxonomy based on the form of the assessment (test, performance assessment, or oral questioning) and whether the scoring was objective (right/wrong) or subjective (based on ratings or qualitative judgment). A newer version of this taxonomy simply lists four assessment methods: selected response, essay, performance assessment, personal communication (Stiggins & Chappuis, 2011, p. 73). This newer version retains the distinction between objective and subjective appraisal for tests, in the two categories of selected and extended (essay) response, and presents performance assessment and personal (oral) communication as single categories with no distinction between objective and subjective appraisal.

In this book, I use a version of Stiggins's older taxonomy that retains the distinction between whether the scoring is objective or subjective. The reason for this decision is that objective (right/wrong) scoring and teacher judgment of the quality of work provide two very different types of feedback to students. Because the focus in this book is on the assessment and further development of higher-order thinking, the type of feedback students get is critical.

Figure 3.1 presents a summary of the "assessment toolkit" used in this book. It describes the methods only as they are used to assess learning. Sometimes these methods can also be used to assess attitudes or interests—for example, using

Figure 3.1 Assessment Options and Their Strengths and Weaknesses

	Right/Wrong Scoring	Judgment-Based Scoring	Most Appropriate Uses	Major Advantages	Potential Pitfalls
Paper-and-pencil tests	Multiple choice, true/false, matching, fill in the blanks	Essays or show-the-work problems judged with rubrics or rating scales	To assess knowledge and thinking over a range of content	Most reliable way to assess knowledge and thinking over a large number of facts and concepts in a content area domain	Require clearly written items that appropriately sample a range of content material; easiest to write recall-level questions
Performance assessments	Judgments of performance on a task using a checklist	Judgments of performance on a task using rubrics, rating scales, and/or with substantive feedback	To assess in-depth thinking in one area *or* to assess skills or products	Allow measurement of in-depth thinking, skills, or products not readily assessable by tests	Require clear expectations for tasks and scoring to provide meaningful assessment information
Oral questions	In-class questions with right/wrong answers	Discussions or interviews evaluated with rubrics, rating scales, and/or with substantive feedback	To assess knowledge and thinking during instruction	Provide feedback for instruction; identify students' concepts and misconceptions	Students may prefer not to speak up or give their honest responses in class
Portfolios	Could use a checklist for portfolio entries but not recommended except for special purposes	Collection of a student's work and reflections over time; entries can be rated separately or as a whole	To document progress or development *or* to showcase achievement	Allow for assessment of student's development and some ownership and control by student	Require clear purpose, focused construction, and long-term attention to give any more useful information than stand-alone assessments

Source: From *The Art and Science of Classroom Assessment: The Missing Part of Pedagogy* (p. 36), by Susan M. Brookhart, 1999, Washington, DC: George Washington University, Graduate School of Education and Human Development. Copyright 1999 by Susan M. Brookhart. Adapted with permission.

paper-and-pencil items in a survey—but this book is strictly about the assessment of learning.

I am not going to discuss all of the methods in Figure 3.1. This book focuses on how to write questions and tasks for the highlighted (shaded) types of assessments. You will use these methods most often to assess higher-order thinking in your classroom. It is important to see how these methods fit with others you might use in this assessment toolkit so that you understand the full range of available options.

Let's take a brief look in this chapter at the whole set of assessment options before exploring in more detail the methods best suited for assessing higher-order thinking. In this context, selecting four of the options to focus on in a book about assessing higher-order thinking should make more sense. As you read the examples of each type of question or task, you should see why some of the kinds of questions and tasks are more suited to assessing higher-order thinking than others.

Formative or Summative?

In the following discussions of each of the assessment options, I refer to how each item is scored. Every assessment question or task needs a method for evaluating the evidence of student learning shown in the student responses. This is *not* the same thing as saying every assessment question or task should be *graded.* You can't tell by looking at the question or task whether it's a formative (for learning) or summative (for grading) assessment. It depends on how the assessment is used, and for the most part the same types of assessments can be used formatively *or* summatively.

Formative assessments are not graded, but you do need to give students feedback on the work, so scoring criteria are still necessary and important. To understand different types of questions and tasks, you need to know how they are appraised. Feedback can take the form of written or oral comments based on the criteria in a rubric, or it can take the form of scoring (as for a quiz) or a "provisional" grade that shows students where they are now, with the understanding that the score or "grade" will change. I recommend using written or oral comments whenever possible.

Summative assessments are assessments of final achievement, and they are graded. You can think of formative uses of various assessment methods as "practice" and summative uses of the same assessment methods as students "showing what they know."

Therefore, think broadly about "scoring" as the appraisal method you will use to turn student responses to questions or tasks into evidence of learning. A student's answer to a question is just marks on a paper until you use some appraisal method to interpret it. If you are willing to use caution and not interpret *scoring* to necessarily mean *grading,* then you are ready to read on as I describe all the available assessment options. Remember to use the examples as demonstrations of how some forms assess higher-order thinking more readily than others.

Paper-and-Pencil Test Items with Right/Wrong Scoring

Collectively, paper-and-pencil test items that can be scored right or wrong, usually by giving one point to a correct answer and no points to an incorrect answer, are called *selected-response items.* The most common kinds are fill-in-the-blank, true/false, matching, and multiple-choice items. All four types can assess recall or comprehension of facts and concepts. Although all four *can* be designed, in some instances, to assess higher-order thinking, for three of them it's a stretch. Multiple-choice items are the kind that you can and should routinely use to assess higher-order thinking.

Fill-in-the-blank items expect a word, phrase, number, or symbol as an answer. They can be questions or problems with blanks for answers, sentences with blanks in them, or a list of elements to identify. They are best at assessing recall, although they can assess simple interpretations and applications. Here is an example of a fill-in item that assesses recall.

> What is the name of the artist who painted the *Mona Lisa*? ________________

True/false items are statements that a student must judge as true or false. Sometimes true/false items take the form of a question that can be answered yes or no, or a computation or sentence that can be judged correct or incorrect. True/false items are a little more flexible in their ability to assess higher-order thinking than fill-in items. They can be statements about relationships, generalizations, predictions, and the like that require more than simple recall to answer. However, they are most often used to assess recall and comprehension. Here is an example of a true/false item that assesses comprehension.

T F The Equal Protection Clause of the Fourteenth Amendment to the Constitution says that individuals must treat each other equally.

Matching exercises give students a list of premises and a list of responses that must be matched according to a principle or criterion described in the directions. They are more flexible in their ability to assess higher-order thinking than fill-in items, but it is very difficult to write good matching exercises that assess more than simple recall. Here is an example of a matching exercise that assesses knowledge of facts.

Match the description of a form of poetry in the first column with its name in the second column.

____ 1. Poem with 3 lines and 17 syllables	a. Cinquain
____ 2. Long narrative poem	b. Epic
____ 3. Five-line poem	c. Haiku
____ 4. Poem with 14 lines and a strict rhyme scheme	d. Ode
	e. Sonnet

Multiple-choice items present students with a stem, usually in the form of a direct question or an incomplete sentence, and then list two or more possible answers. The student must choose the correct answer. Multiple-choice items are much maligned because they are associated with high-stakes tests and with recall-level assessment. It is true that multiple-choice items can be overused, but it is not true that they can assess only recall-level thinking. Part of my reason for writing this book is to show you how to use multiple-choice items to assess higher-order thinking as well. A real advantage of multiple-choice items is that you can assess higher-order thinking and still assess a broader range of content than you can with essay test items or performance assessments, because a student can complete many multiple-choice items in the time it takes to write one essay or do a performance assessment task.

To give you a preview of how this works, let's compare two multiple-choice items. The first one assesses recall of a fact in literature.

In E. B. White's essay "Twins," which character gives birth to twins?

A. The speaker's mother
B. A cow moose
C. A red deer
D. A shoe clerk

The second example is a multiple-choice item that assesses higher-order thinking in the same content area.

The following is from the first paragraph of the essay "Twins."

They stood there, mother and child, under a gray beech whose trunk was engraved with dozens of hearts and initials.

What does the sentence imply?

A. E. B. White is sympathetic to parents and children.
B. The deer were hiding from E. B. White and the other sightseers.
C. E. B. White is aware of both nature and the urban setting.
D. The graffiti interferes with E. B. White's enjoyment of the scene.

Source: National Assessment of Educational Progress (NAEP) released items: 2011, grade 8, block R2, question #8.

The student would need to know the same fact—which character gives birth to twins—in order to respond to this question, but she would also need to think about the meaning of that fact in the context of E. B. White's observations about his trip to the zoo. The student would need to comprehend the plain English meaning of the sentence, comprehend the larger essay (which is about a trip to the Bronx Zoo and what the author observed), and also understand some of the rhetorical devices the author used to make a point about the irony of such a natural event taking place in the middle of a crowded city, and that he ended the essay not with cynicism or criticism of urban children's lack of appreciation for nature, which might be expected, but rather with a sense of wonder. Given all that, choice C is the correct answer. Without knowing all that and using that knowledge to interpret the sentence, all four of the choices are reasonable.

If you doubt this, allow me to give some personal testimony. As I was writing this section of the book, I looked on the NAEP released-item website, which is a gold mine of examples of test questions, and found this one. I'm reasonably well-read, plus I'm an expert in assessment and have written hundreds of multiple-choice questions. I know how they work. This is an 8th grade question—how tough could it be? *But I chose the wrong answer.* Intrigued, I obtained a copy of the essay itself and read it and thought about both the contents of the essay and what the author was trying to accomplish with it. Then, and only then, the question made sense to me, and I was able to do the think-aloud that ended up being the explanation in the previous paragraph. Point proven: this question requires higher-order thinking.

Chapter 4 will show you how to write multiple-choice items that assess higher-order thinking. I encourage you to do this regularly. Also, point out to your students that these multiple-choice items are actually assessing thinking. Many of the state, national, and international tests they will take use this kind of question. In my opinion, multiple-choice questions that assess higher-order thinking are underused in regular classroom assessment and represent a huge opportunity to infuse more higher-order thinking into classroom assessment. I hope, after you read Chapter 4, that you will agree.

Paper-and-Pencil Test Items with Judgment-Based Scoring

Paper-and-pencil test items that require students to produce, not choose, an answer are called *constructed-response items.* The two most common kinds are essay test questions and show-the-work math problems. Teachers use rubrics or other point schemes to indicate the quality of the response, usually on a scale with several points or quality levels. Unlike right/wrong test items, where anyone who uses the same scoring key would come up with the same score, different teachers might disagree on the quality of a student's response. The goal is to write a clear enough question and use a clear enough rubric that the amount of disagreement is minimal.

Constructed-response questions can, *but should not,* be used to assess recall. For example, you could ask students to list four states of matter found on Earth and their definitions. This is a waste of student time and effort because you could more easily and quickly find out if students knew these facts with selected-response questions. Here is an example of an essay test question that asks students to apply their knowledge of the states of matter to solve a problem.

> Your science lab team discovers an unknown substance, and your teacher asks you to discover whether it is a solid, a liquid, or a gas. How could you do that?

In this example, the problem is given, but students must design the means to solve it. Their designs will show their knowledge of scientific reasoning as well as of states of matter. Students' answers to this question would be scored with a rubric or a point scheme.

Words are not the only medium in which students can construct answers. They can also use numbers, musical notation, computer code, or any other symbol system, depending on the subject matter and what is to be assessed. Here is an example of a constructed-response mathematics problem.

> Peter is making meat and cheese sandwiches for his class picnic. He has white bread and wheat bread; ham, roast beef, and turkey; and American cheese and Swiss cheese. How many different kinds of sandwiches can he make? Show your work and explain your reasoning.

Chapter 5 will show you how to write effective questions for three purposes: essay questions on tests, show-the-work problems, and open-ended questions that will help you use classroom discussions as opportunities for formative assessment. Questions for all of these purposes should require students to think and to make their thinking visible in their responses.

Performance Assessments

Performance assessments require students to do something—to create a product, to demonstrate a performance, or both. Performance assessments have two parts: the performance task and the criteria or scoring scheme by which the performance will be evaluated. Both are required. In this book, I concentrate on how to design and write the performance task, and I focus on performance tasks that assess higher-order thinking and require judgment-based scoring.

Performance assessments with right/wrong scoring are usually simple demonstrations of what students can do. Performance assessments that can be scored right or wrong, or as a series of yes/no decisions on a checklist, typically assess recall or the execution of simple skills. Here are two examples of this kind of performance assessment:

- The teacher asks each student to count by 5s to 100.
- Each student follows a checklist to pack a first aid kit suitable for home use.

Even though these are performance assessments, they do not require higher-order thinking. Performance assessments with right/wrong scoring are an important method to keep in the assessment toolkit; however, in this book I focus on designing and writing complex performance assessments that require more than right/wrong scoring.

Performance assessments with judgment-based scoring are usually complex performances that align with learning objectives at higher cognitive levels than the simple performances just described. The trick is to make both the task *and the scoring* reflect higher-order thinking. Consider the following example of a performance task.

Working in groups of four, devise a class survey to collect information about students that could be displayed in a bar graph. Think of the kinds of information that would work for this purpose: kinds of pets, favorite ice cream flavors, and so on. You can ask about one or more things. Put items on your survey that you really think would be interesting to know about. Survey the whole class. When your group has its surveys back, tally the data as a group. Then, individually, each student will write his or her own report describing (1) what you did and why, and (2) what you found out. In the section about what you found out, display the results for each question you asked in a bar graph. Finally, close with a section describing (3) what you learned from doing this survey.

This is a complex performance task. It asks students to define their own problem (What do we want to know that lends itself to a bar graph display?). The means to answering the question is prescribed (a survey), but the questions for the report sections are open-ended. Students will have many different reasons for what they wanted to know and what they think they learned either about the content of the report or about making surveys and bar graphs. Students' descriptions of what they did and learned should contain rich evidence about what they do (and don't) understand about bar graphs as a mathematical tool and as a reporting and communication mechanism.

A scoring scheme that focused merely on the correctness of the bar graphs would squander information about the students' thought processes and their understanding of the use of bar graphs for conveying certain kinds of information. Once the reports were sent home and only the scores remained, there would be no information about students' thinking in this regard. This is the reason that a performance assessment has *two* parts, the task and the scoring scheme, even though the focus in this book is on the first part—designing and writing the tasks.

Oral Questions

Oral questions can take the form of an oral exam or interview, in which case they can be written in a manner similar to that of constructed-response questions for an essay test. However, oral questions are also useful for more informal in-class formative assessment. Oral questioning of students, whether in whole-class or small-group discussion, opens a window into students' understanding. Plus, oral questioning in a discussion setting allows students to respond to one another's ideas and build on one another's thinking.

Oral questions with right/wrong feedback are recall questions that are easy to ask "on the fly." This is the kind of question teachers ask most often when they don't prepare the questions ahead of time. Typically, the teacher asks a question of one student at a time, then responds "yes" or "right" or something like that so that the student and the rest of the class know the fact was correct. Here are two examples:

- What is the capital of Virginia?
- How many electrons are in an atom of helium?

Such questions are not a good use of oral questioning time. If students must know certain facts for a particular learning outcome, a brief quiz is a more efficient way to find out what they know. I mention this kind of question only because this chapter covers the whole range of assessment options, and oral questions with right/wrong feedback are possible and, once in a while, even useful. If you are going to ask students this kind of question, consider using methods that ask all the students, not just the one you call on, so that you have a sense of the whole class's knowledge. Clickers and whiteboards are two response mechanisms that allow the whole class to respond. But really, if you have to remember one thing from this paragraph, it's best to remember *not* to ask this kind of question very often.

Oral questions with judgment-based feedback are best for revealing student thinking so that others can comment on it. Oral questions that require students to think are typically open-ended questions that allow for more than one answer. Students' responses will give you insight not only into *what* they are thinking but also into *how* they are understanding the concepts under study.

It's best to keep three things in mind when you use open-ended oral questions with students. One, you must prepare the questions ahead of time, as part of regular lesson planning. No matter how well you think on your feet, you simply will not arrive at high-quality open-ended questions that appropriately sample the intended domains of learning on the fly. It doesn't work that way. Two, before you give students feedback on their answers, take the opportunity to have students respond to one another: "Aaron, can you add something to Zach's idea?" "Leiah, do you agree with Amir's point, and can you tell us why?" Three, your feedback to students should be substantive, based on criteria—that is, qualities you are looking for in student understanding that signal the students' progress toward the learning target—and nonjudgmental. In short, it should exhibit all the characteristics of effective feedback (Brookhart, 2008), just as feedback on other types of work would.

Chapter 5 goes into detail about how to write open-ended questions that are useful for class discussion and that simultaneously yield both learning and formative assessment information. For now, here are just a couple of examples:

- Why do you think we define an ecosystem as a community with both living and nonliving components? Can you give an example of how the two are related in the greater Yellowstone ecosystem?
- Why is the concept of *slope* so important? We're spending a lot of time on it—what kinds of problems in the world will slope help us understand?

Portfolios

Some educators consider portfolios a type of performance assessment, which is true. To my way of thinking, they are a special kind of performance assessment, and they have enough unique characteristics that it is worth talking about them separately. Because this book concentrates on how to design and write performance assessment tasks, I won't go into detail here about designing portfolios—which you can think of as a collection of tasks. As I do for some of the other methods, I include portfolios here for the sake of completeness. It's important to know the whole range of assessment options you can use.

Portfolios fall into two general categories: growth portfolios and best-work portfolios (Brookhart & Nitko, 2015). Growth portfolios show development, whereas best-work portfolios showcase student accomplishments. In general, but not always, growth portfolios are best for formative assessment purposes, and best-work portfolios are best for summative assessment purposes (grading).

Portfolios with right/wrong scoring are portfolios that are scored with a checklist of required elements. Although this approach is possible, it is not recommended. The idea of right/wrong or checklist scoring runs counter to the usual purpose for constructing portfolios in the first place: accumulating and evaluating a body of evidence to make some claims about student learning.

Portfolios with judgment-based scoring or feedback are portfolios in which the body of evidence contained in the portfolio is judged against criteria for learning, typically with rubrics. Portfolios typically include self-reflection or self-assessment, either piece-by-piece or overall. This self-assessment can be guided by open-ended questions (e.g., "What did you learn from doing this piece?") or by rubrics. Teacher assessment of the portfolio can use rubrics or feedback comments, or both. Sometimes each piece of evidence is assessed with its own rubric.

Sometimes the portfolio contents as a whole are assessed with an overall rubric. At other times, most often with growth portfolios, no rubric or scoring scheme is used. Rather, the teacher gives feedback based on criteria.

Here are examples of a growth portfolio and a best-work portfolio:

- **A growth portfolio in writing to demonstrate development in several genres.** Students include brainstorming, first draft, feedback, and final draft for an expository piece from the beginning of the school year and the end of the year. They also include examples of finished narrative, persuasive, and imaginative writing, of their choice, for a total of six writing examples. Each piece is captioned with a sticky note on which the student tells what the piece demonstrates about the writing. The final entry is an end-of-year essay titled "What I Learned About Writing This Year."
- **A best-work portfolio in mathematics to demonstrate learning outcomes in understanding ratios, rates, and proportions.** Students must include two examples of completed problem sets (homework or classwork) with teacher feedback, one quiz, and the unit test. They annotate each of these with a reflection telling what the piece shows they know and can do. Students must also create two original word problems using ratios, rates, or proportions; ask a family member or classmate to solve them; and write what feedback they would give to the problem solver. Finally, they must include a one-page essay titled "What Is a Ratio and Why Is It Important to Know?"

Assessment Options That Work Best for Higher-Order Thinking

In the next five chapters, I focus on designing and writing just four of the assessment methods in the toolkit: multiple-choice questions, open-ended questions for both essays and oral questioning, and performance tasks. Because performance tasks can assess skills or processes, can be large or small in scope, and can vary significantly in the amount of structure they give students and the level of cognitive functioning they require, I devote three chapters to designing and writing performance tasks.

These formats are *not* the only assessment formats; rather, they are the ones most commonly (and successfully) used to assess higher-order thinking. If you want to read more about how to design and write assessment items and tasks in the other formats—fill-in-the-blank, true/false, matching, or portfolios—you can consult a standard assessment textbook (e.g., Brookhart & Nitko, 2015; Stiggins & Chappuis, 2011).

4 Multiple-Choice Questions That Assess Higher-Order Thinking

Contrary to popular belief, multiple-choice questions can assess higher-order thinking skills, most often at the Analyze level and sometimes at the Evaluate level (although not at the Create level; by definition, a selected-response question cannot ask students to create something). Such questions typically rely on introductory material of some sort. They are useful not only for tests but also for classroom-response systems ("clickers"), formative assessment strategies that have students choose an answer and then debate it with those who disagree, and the like. They have the advantage of not requiring a lot of student writing, which is useful for assessing students who have poor writing skills but who can, when asked, apply higher-order thinking skills to content-area learning.

This chapter focuses on how to write multiple-choice questions that assess higher-order thinking, in keeping with the book's purpose of describing how to write questions and tasks. It does not discuss how to put such questions together to make a meaningful test. Appendix A shows how to do that by using a test blueprint. Nor does this chapter focus on how to write multiple-choice questions that assess students' abilities to recall facts or comprehend concepts. You will probably use recall-level multiple-choice questions in your classroom, but you will find it more of a challenge to write questions that assess higher-order thinking.

Guidelines for Writing Multiple-Choice Questions

A multiple-choice question is made up of one or more introductory sentences, called the *stem,* and two or more response choices. Students must select the response choice that best answers the question posed by the stem. All multiple-choice items, whether they assess higher-order thinking, recall, or comprehension, should ask a direct question or present a specific problem for students to answer. Multiple-choice questions should be written in ordinary language accessible to all students, not language that sounds like it comes from a textbook. Vocabulary and sentence structure should be simple, and there should be one correct or best answer. One response choice should be an unambiguous correct answer for students who understand the content being assessed. Each response choice should be plausible to students who do not understand the content being assessed in the question. The plausibility principle extends both to content (e.g., if a question asks about an insect, all the choices should be insects) and to grammar and usage clues that make one answer obviously correct without students needing to think about the content.

There are several types of multiple-choice questions. Two that are particularly useful for our purposes are *correct-answer* and *best-answer* multiple-choice questions. I'll show you simple examples first that do not require higher-order thinking.

Correct-answer questions have one correct answer, and the other choices are demonstrably incorrect. Here is an example that requires thinking at the Apply level of Bloom's taxonomy.

Solve for x: $2(x + 2) = 16$

A. 4
B. 6 *
C. 7
D. 8

This question has one correct answer. Only the number 6 makes the equation true.

Best-answer items have several partially correct answers, but only one response choice is most arguably the best. The following example requires thinking at the Understand level of Bloom's taxonomy.

Which of the following kinds of organizations would most likely be involved in protecting people's rights to have a safe workplace?

A. A political party
B. A parent-teacher association
C. A labor union *
D. A charity

Source: National Assessment of Educational Progress (NAEP) released items: 2010, grade 4, block C4, question #10.

In this question, any of the organizations listed as response choices might, on occasion, be involved in protecting people's rights to have a safe workplace; however, the organization most likely to be involved is a labor union (C).

People have criticized multiple-choice items for many reasons. Probably the most important one is that students do not have a chance to create or express their own solutions to the problem the question poses. This is a fair criticism, but it is offset by the breadth of learning objectives that multiple-choice questions can assess in a short period of time. In one testing period, students cannot give extended written answers with original justifications for very many questions. However, a set of well-crafted multiple-choice items with introductory material can, in the same amount of time as is required to respond to one or two essay questions, assess students' thinking about a whole range of learning objectives.

By their nature, multiple-choice items still require questions that have one correct or best answer. Therefore, multiple-choice questions cannot assess divergent thinking in the same way as constructed-response (essay) questions or performance assessments can. But they can assess thinking at cognitive levels such as Analyze and Evaluate. To do this, create multiple-choice items that have introductory material—that is, questions that give students something to think *about*.

Multiple-Choice Questions with Introductory Material

This kind of multiple-choice question has several names, including *context-dependent items* and *items with introductory material.* The idea is that you base your multiple-choice question on a scenario, chart, graph, map, text excerpt, cartoon, or other material that you present to the student right before the question. The multiple-choice question can then focus on the student's analysis or evaluation of the material, not whether or not the student can recall a bit of text, map, or chart from memory. In the following example, the reading passage serves as introductory material. Students do not need to have memorized a story; the passage is there for them to read. The multiple-choice question then is able to tap how well students can make inferences from the material, not how well they can remember something they read.

Here is a puzzle. See if you can solve it.

These are things that have two wings and fly. They are much smaller than airplanes, and they are alive. Sometimes these things make a lot of noise with their chirping and singing. All of them have feathers, and they come in different colors. What are these?

A. Birds *
B. Butterflies
C. Horseflies
D. Jet airplanes

Source: National Assessment of Educational Progress (NAEP) released items: 2008, age 9, block R28, question #7.

You can demonstrate for yourself that this question requires students to use higher-order thinking by applying the strategy from Chapter 2: from the student's point of view, what problem needs to be solved here? *The directions tell me to solve a puzzle. When I read the passage, I have to identify the nature of that puzzle: it's a riddle. To answer the question "What are these?" I have to select from the passage all the things that describe the unidentified objects in question ("these"), and then frame the problem as "Which of these choices is defined by all of these descriptions from the passage?"*

These tasks are what make this question tap Analyze-level thinking: the student is identifying parts of the passage (the descriptions) and using them to solve the problem.

Putting your teacher hat back on, the "reason-like-a-student" strategy has just given you evidence that the question addresses the Common Core standard on "refer[ring] to details and examples in a text when explaining what the text says explicitly and when drawing inferences from the text" (CCSS.ELA-LITERACY.RL.4.1). Thinking through what the question is actually asking helps you see and explain the match.

Designing Multiple-Choice Questions with Introductory Material

To design multiple-choice questions with introductory material to which students must apply higher-order thinking, first identify exactly what content knowledge and skills and what level of thinking you want to assess. This advice should be sounding familiar by now. This is the first step in designing *any* kind of assessment.

Second, identify the material (text, chart, graph, picture, map, whatever) that students will think about. Make this choice consistent with your assessment purpose. For example, if you want to assess whether students can use a map key, you might want to start with a map that has a key, or maybe a map that doesn't have a key but needs one. If you want to assess whether students can interpret a line graph, use a line graph as your introductory material.

Third—and this is the part that most teachers find the hardest—write a multiple-choice question that requires analyzing or evaluating the introductory material. For an example, let's use our map-key question. If you ask, "What symbol is used for capital cities?" and right in the key there is an entry reading "capital city" with a star beside it, you are assessing comprehension. That's not a bad thing to assess, but in this chapter we're learning to write multiple-choice questions that tap more than comprehension. If you ask, "How many capital cities are on the map?"

you are assessing comprehension, or at most application. It's a one-step problem solved by counting the number of stars on the map.

To write a question that requires Analyze-level thinking, ask students to make inferences that can be supported with information in the introductory material but require drawing conclusions using logic and, usually, additional background knowledge. Suppose our map was a map of the United States, with each state's capital marked, as in the following task.

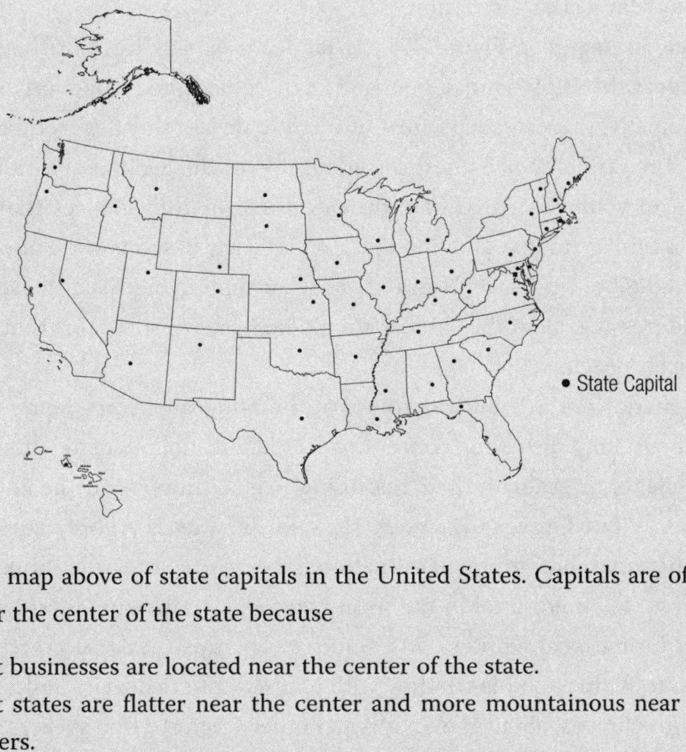

Look at the map above of state capitals in the United States. Capitals are often located near the center of the state because

A. Most businesses are located near the center of the state.
B. Most states are flatter near the center and more mountainous near the borders.
C. The climate is usually milder near the center of the state.
D. It is easier for people from around the state to reach a central location. *

Source: National Assessment of Educational Progress (NAEP) released items: 2010, grade 4, block G3, question #12.

Be careful. The question posed in this task is an Analyze-level question *only if* students have not learned the fact that capitals in central locations make transportation easier, either from a textbook or from a class discussion or exercise. A common trap for teachers writing a multiple-choice or any other kind of question is to think they have written an Analyze-level question when, in fact, they are testing only recall. Discovering that central locations are useful for state capitals requires Analyze-level thinking, but once the discovery is made, remembering requires only recall. You may think you are assessing the C3 dimension "Applying disciplinary concepts and tools" (NCSS, 2013) when in fact you are simply assessing recall of last Thursday's class discussion.

The strategies in Figure 4.1 are far from exhaustive, but they will give you some ideas. Multiple-choice questions can be designed using any of these strategies. Actually, you can adapt most of them to design short essay questions, too. To design a multiple-choice question, adapt one of the general questions in the third column to your content. Then, provide three or four choices that are plausible and of a similar nature, and one that is clearly the best answer. For example, if you presented a political speech and asked what underlying issue the speaker seemed to be addressing, all of the choices should be issues of some sort that could prompt a political speech.

Scenarios are a good way to set up thinking questions. Some types are particularly useful. For testing content, stories about fictional students can invite the real students to evaluate their reasoning (e.g., "Aubrey said the cork would float because.... But Grover disagreed. He said.... Why is Aubrey correct?"). Stories about fictional, but common, situations also invite students' thinking (e.g., "Mr. Brown wrote an editorial in the local newspaper criticizing local business people for not hiring local workers. Ms. Smith, who runs the local greeting card store, threw a rock through his window with a nasty note tied to it," followed by a question, with choices, about the First Amendment right to free speech). Scenarios are a bread-and-butter strategy for mathematics word problems, but we are less likely to think of using them in other disciplines. It's time to change that limited perspective. A great thing about both fictional students and other scenarios is that you can control all the variables, leaving out extraneous information and focusing tightly on the concept and thinking skills you want to assess.

Figure 4.1 Idea Bank: Strategies for Assessing Higher-Order Thinking with Multiple-Choice Questions

To Assess	Present This Material	Ask This Question
Identify issues or problems	A text, speech, problem, policy, political cartoon, or experiment and results	• What is the main issue? • What is the problem?
Analyze arguments	A text, speech, or experimental design	• What evidence does the author give that . . . ? • What is the most credible piece of evidence that . . . ? • On what assumptions does this argument rest?
Compare and contrast	Two texts, events, scenarios, concepts, characters, or principles	• Which elements in [text] are like [or not like] . . . ? • Ask for a generalization based on similarities or differences.
Evaluate materials and methods for their intended purposes	A text, speech, policy, theory, experimental design, or work of art	• What was the author trying to accomplish? • What elements in the work [accomplish some purpose]? • How well does the author [accomplish some purpose]?
Make or evaluate a deductive conclusion	A statement or premise	• What conclusion follows logically? • What counterexample would make this statement untrue?
Make or evaluate an inductive conclusion	Information in the form of a scenario, graph, table, chart, or list	• What conclusion follows logically? • What else must be true?
Evaluate the credibility of a source	A scenario, speech, advertisement, website, or other source of information	• Is this information believable? • Why is this information believable [or not]?
Identify or evaluate implicit assumptions	An argument, speech, or explanation that has some implicit assumptions	• What must be assumed in order for this argument to make sense? • Which of the following assumptions [from the argument] is the most [or least] credible?
Identify or evaluate rhetorical and persuasive strategies	A speech, advertisement, editorial, or other persuasive communication	• What is the author trying to persuade readers [viewers] to do [think]? • How persuasive would [some aspect] be with [some audience]? • What imagery [or other strategy] is intended to persuade the audience [to do or think something]?
Reason with data	A text, cartoon, graph, data table, or chart and a problem that requires this information for its solution	• Solve the problem. • Identify the key information needed for solving the problem.

Source: From *How to Assess Higher-Order Thinking Skills in Your Classroom* (pp. 144–147), by Susan M. Brookhart, 2010, Alexandria, VA: ASCD. Copyright 2010 by ASCD. The figure has been modified to focus on multiple-choice questions with introductory material.

Also note that the list of strategies in Figure 4.1 is general, for use in any discipline. The strategies must be used with specific content in order to generate useful questions. The remainder of this chapter gives several examples in a few different subject areas. The idea is not for me to write your questions for you or to illustrate all the possible types of questions that could be asked. Rather, the purpose of the examples is to give you some inspiration and ideas for creating multiple-choice questions that will assess higher-order thinking in your own teaching.

Language Arts Example

We have already seen an example of a language arts question about making an inference in elementary-level reading. The following is an example of a question that requires high school students to analyze some text and draw a conclusion.

In Act 3, Scene 2 of Shakespeare's *Julius Caesar*, Brutus explains why he killed Caesar. Here is an excerpt from that speech:

> If there be any in this assembly, any dear friend of Caesar's, to him I say, that Brutus' love to Caesar was no less than his. If then that friend demand why Brutus rose against Caesar, this is my answer: —Not that I loved Caesar less, but that I loved Rome more. Had you rather Caesar were living and die all slaves, than that Caesar were dead, to live all free men? As Caesar loved me, I weep for him; as he was fortunate, I rejoice at it; as he was valiant, I honour him: but, as he was ambitious, I slew him.

Brutus delivered his speech in the Forum in front of citizens. What do you think Brutus wanted the citizens to think as a result of hearing him speak?

A. Brutus had mixed feelings about Caesar and is not sure he should have killed him.
B. Brutus killed Caesar because Caesar was ambitious and self-centered.
C. Killing Caesar was justified because Caesar's self-interest was harming citizens. *

From the point of view of the student, here is the thinking process: *What problem am I being asked to solve? I am asked to draw a conclusion from reading a speech. The conclusion I draw should be the speaker's intended message to his audience. I will need to add background knowledge about the author's purpose, word choice, tone, and so on—literary elements I have been learning about as we read the play. I will need to identify elements in the speech and reason with them to draw a conclusion about the author's message.*

Identifying parts and reasoning from them is what places the task at the Analyze level of thinking. Thinking through the "problem to solve" from a student's point of view shows that the question aligns with the Common Core standard on "determin[ing] the meaning of words and phrases as they are used in the text, including figurative and connotative meanings; analyz[ing] the impact of specific word choices on meaning and tone, including words with multiple meanings or language that is particularly fresh, engaging, or beautiful. (Include Shakespeare as well as other authors.)" (CCSS.ELA-LITERACY.RL.11-12.4).

Mathematics Examples

The Shakespeare question asked students to use inductive reasoning. The following mathematics task asks students to reason by analogy.

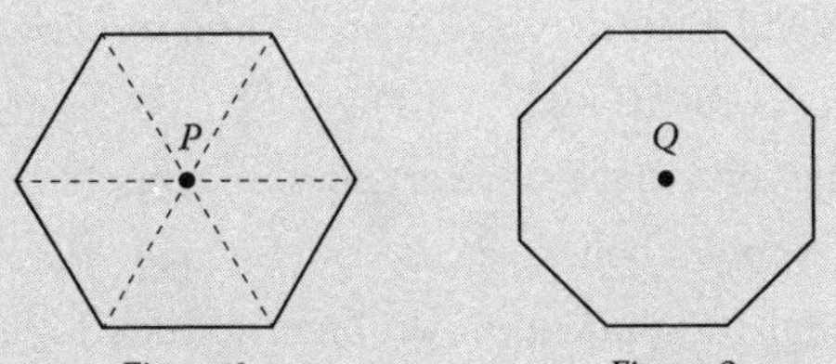

Figure 1 Figure 2

Figure 1 is a regular hexagon with its center at point *P*. The dotted lines divide the hexagon completely into 6 congruent triangles sharing a vertex at point *P*.

Figure 2 is a regular octagon with its center at point *Q*. The octagon can be completely divided into congruent triangles sharing a vertex at point *Q*.

This division could produce

A. 16 congruent equilateral triangles.
B. 16 congruent isosceles triangles.
C. 8 congruent right triangles.
D. 8 congruent equilateral triangles.
E. 8 congruent isosceles triangles. *

Source: National Assessment of Educational Progress (NAEP) released items: 2011, grade 8, block M8, question #13.

Here is the thinking from the student's point of view: *What problem is this question asking me to solve? I need to describe what will happen when I divide the octagon into congruent triangles. I need some content knowledge—for example, the meanings of* regular, congruent, equilateral, isosceles, *and so on. I need to be able to describe what happens when the hexagon is divided and apply the same reasoning to dividing the octagon.*

The teacher can see that this question aligns with Common Core standards on using physical models, transparencies, or geometry software to understand congruence and similarity (CCSS.MATH.CONTENT.8.G.A), reasoning abstractly and quantitatively (CCSS.MATH.PRACTICE.MP2), and looking for and making use of structure (CCSS.MATH.PRACTICE.MP7).

This problem has one right answer, so some might argue that the level of thinking required is Apply. I believe a case can be made that this problem requires Analyze-level thinking. In application problems, students apply a strategy or an algorithm they have been taught ("Here's how to calculate slope"). In this problem, the students must look at the hexagon, learn from it what such a division looks like, and apply to the octagon the strategy they worked out themselves on the hexagon. Analyzing the hexagon example, then reasoning by analogy to the octagon, is what makes this problem an example of Analyze-level thinking.

Multiple-choice questions can also ask about the problem-solving process itself. In the following problem, students are asked to identify missing information.

Armand walked for 8 minutes from his house to Mateo's house. He spent 25 minutes at Mateo's house. He walked 9 minutes to the store. He bought baseball cards at the store. He walked 10 more minutes to get home.

What one additional piece of information is needed to find how many minutes Armand was away from his house?

A. What time Armand left home
B. How fast Armand walked
C. How far Armand's house is from Mateo's house
D. How long Armand was at the store *

Here is this problem from the student's point of view: *What is this problem asking me to do? It is asking me to identify missing information, of course, but what must I do to do that? I have to identify the problem (it's an addition problem). I have to identify separate data points (the numbers I will add) in the problem and figure out which one is missing.*

Identifying the parts in the problem and reasoning with them requires thinking at the Analyze level. To succeed at this task, students need to be able to fulfill the Common Core standard of "solv[ing] multistep word problems posed with whole numbers and having whole-number answers using the four operations" (CCSS.MATH.CONTENT.4.OA.A3) as well as to make sense of problems and persevere in solving them (CCSS.MATH.PRACTICE.MP1), reason abstractly and quantitatively (CCSS.MATH.PRACTICE.MP2), and construct viable arguments and critique the reasoning of others (CCSS.MATH.PRACTICE.MP3).

Science Examples

The following is an example of a 12th grade question that students did not find very difficult. Eighty-eight percent of students nationally answered this question correctly. Yet it does require higher-order thinking. We'll have more to say about the difference between level of thinking and difficulty in Chapter 8, but it's worth foreshadowing now as you think your way through various examples. The length and complexity of a question contribute to its difficulty, but they do not determine it completely.

A student took a sample of water from a pond and examined it under a microscope. She identified several species of protozoans, including two species of *Paramecium* that are known to eat the same food. The student decided to examine the water sample every day for a week. She added food for the *Paramecia* each day and counted the number of each species. Her findings are summarized in the table below.

NUMBER OF *PARAMECIA* IN POND WATER SAMPLE

Day	Species *S*	Species *T*
1	50	50
2	60	80
3	100	90
4	150	60
5	160	50
6	160	30
7	160	20

Which of the following can be correctly concluded from the data?

A. Species *S* is the food for species *T*.
B. Species *T* is more common than species *S*.
C. Species *S* is a more successful competitor than species *T*. *
D. Species *T* is a more successful competitor than species *S*.

Source: National Assessment of Educational Progress (NAEP) released items: 2005, grade 12, block S14, question #5.

Here's the problem from the student's point of view: *What is this problem asking me to do? I must draw a conclusion. To do that, I need to understand how the experiment was designed, read the data table correctly, and then look for patterns in the data that could answer the question. I also need some background knowledge about experimental design and about how species compete for food in an ecosystem.*

These problem-solving and knowledge requirements could have produced a very difficult question, but they did not. I think this question was not difficult because of the simple experimental design and the clear pattern in the data. Nevertheless, the question requires thinking at the Analyze level.

Like the previous problem, the following 4th grade problem requires higher-order thinking in science. However, it is much more difficult. Nationally, only 35 percent of students chose the correct answer.

A student wants to know whether two cups hold the same volume of water. The two cups have different weights (masses).

Cup 1 *Cup 2*

The student completely fills Cup 1 with water. The student wants to measure if Cup 2 holds the same volume of water. What should the student do next to complete the measurements?

A. Completely fill Cup 2 with water and then look at the cups side by side.
B. Pour half of the water from Cup 1 into Cup 2, weigh each cup, and then compare their weights.
C. Pour all of the water from Cup 1 into Cup 2 to see if the water completely fills Cup 2 without spilling over. *
D. Completely fill Cup 2 with water, weigh each filled cup, and then compare the weights.

Source: National Assessment of Educational Progress (NAEP) released items: 2009, grade 4, block S7, question #12.

From a student's point of view, what is this problem asking? *I must design a procedure that would answer the question about the volume of Cup 2. I must use scientific reasoning to do this and make sure I do not confound my procedure with extraneous factors like the weight of the cups. To do this, I need background knowledge about units of measure and about how to measure.*

If this were an open-ended question—if it did not have the set of multiple-choice responses—it would require thinking at the Create level, because students would have to design a valid procedure. In this multiple-choice version, students must think at the Evaluate level; they must evaluate the procedures that are listed and select the most valid one.

Both of these science examples use rather long introductory material. When you set up such a scenario, you can use it with several multiple-choice questions or with a mixture of multiple-choice and short constructed-response questions. For example, for the paramecium scenario, you might ask students to speculate on other variables that might be tested (e.g., the temperature of the water) before the conclusion that Species *S* is more successful can be stated more definitely, and design an experiment that would test the effects of these variables. Then you would have a multiple-choice question and a companion short-essay question using the same scenario.

Social Studies Example

Questions that set up a problem to which students must apply higher-order thinking do not need to be long. Consider the following problem in high school economics.

How would a large increase in the number of business and personal bankruptcies over several years tend to affect the interest rates that banks charge for loans?

A. Interest rates would fall because the supply of funds would decrease.
B. Interest rates would rise because banks would find it riskier to lend funds. *
C. Interest rates would stay the same because banks are not affected by bankruptcies.
D. The answer cannot be determined because the government sets interest rates that banks charge for loans.

Source: National Assessment of Educational Progress (NAEP) released items: 2012, grade 12, block E5, question #11.

Once again, let's look at this problem from the student's point of view: *What is this problem asking me to do? I must make a prediction. To do this, I need to know some facts and concepts about business and personal bankruptcies and about loan procedures and interest rates. I must apply what I know to the scenario and draw a conclusion about the result.*

The stem in this question sets up a scenario in the form of a hypothetical situation—and does it with one sentence. The scenario is that there are a large number of bankruptcies, and the students are asked to draw a conclusion based on what they know about economic forces. This requires thinking at the Analyze level.

Of course, social studies questions, too, can have more elaborate introductory material. Asking students to interpret maps and graphs, historical and political speeches, or artifacts like photographs, posters, or political cartoons requires presenting students with introductory material and then posing one or more questions that call for some sort of Analyze- or Evaluate-level thinking. As with the science examples, introductory material can be used with more than one question and with more than one question format.

Arts Examples

Finally, here are a couple of examples from the arts. The first is a visual arts example.

What is the main compositional element in this painting?

A. Linear perspective
B. Horizontal emphasis *
C. Vertical emphasis
D. Foreshortening

Let's consider it from the point of view of the student: *This question is asking me to look at elements of the painting (e.g., the cows, the mountains) and decide how*

they are composed, or put together for visual effect. I need some background knowledge about the principles of composition and their names (e.g., perspective*). I also need viewing skills, presumably developed by analyzing other paintings, which allow me to identify examples of those compositional principles when I see them. Then I need to analyze the elements of this specific painting according to the compositional principles.*

All art forms can be analyzed, not just paintings. The following example is a question calling for analysis of a musical composition. I selected this example because it illustrates using diagrams instead of words as the response options in a multiple-choice question.

The next piece of music will be used for question 2. The music will be played one time. Before you hear the music, read question 2.

[Music played: "The Art of the Fugue, BMV 1080" by Johann Sebastian Bach. Musical selection is not reproduced in this book.]

Which diagram best illustrates the texture of the music?

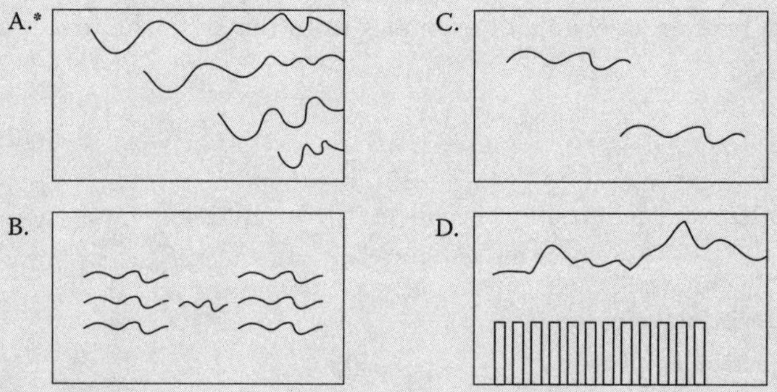

Source: National Assessment of Educational Progress (NAEP) released items: 2008, grade 8, block A4, question #2.

From the student's point of view, here is what this question is asking: *This question is asking me to diagram what I hear. That means I need to hear separately each voice in the recording, so that I can make a line for each one. Finally, I have to represent my understanding of how the piece is composed in a two-dimensional diagram with time on the X-axis and each voice represented with a line.*

Because I can't "show" you the music, let me tell you that this fugue starts with one line of music that rises and falls roughly like the top line in the diagram that starts farthest to the left in choice A. Three additional voices join, one at a time, playing approximately the same line of music that the first player played. That's why choice A is correct.

Inspiration?

How do you feel about the much-maligned multiple-choice question now? I hope this chapter has persuaded you that multiple-choice questions can test important content and higher-order thinking, and has given you some resources to do this. The kinds of multiple-choice questions presented in this chapter are harder to write than the kinds that ask something such as "Who was the first president of the United States?" but they are well worth the effort. I recommend you use several questions like this every time you give a multiple-choice test. Use a test blueprint such as the one in Appendix A to make sure the balance of content and thinking skills assessed by your test matches your intentions.

I also recommend you use individual questions like these to get students thinking during class discussions. You can have students talk with one another about the reasoning behind their choices and why the correct answer is correct and the other choices are not. You can also have students analyze the question itself, similar to the way I did after each of the examples (*What is this question asking me to do?*) to help develop their problem-identification and problem-solving skills.

Some readers may be wondering why I used so many examples from the National Assessment of Educational Progress (NAEP). Released items from NAEP (http://nces.ed.gov/nationsreportcard/about/naeptools.aspx, select "Questions Tool") are in the public domain and are one of the best sources I know for multiple-choice items that require higher-order thinking—better, for example, than many released multiple-choice items from state tests or multiple-choice items that come with textbooks (although there are some wonderful *constructed-response* released items from state tests and from textbooks that do require higher-order thinking). I encourage you to play around with the NAEP Questions Tool as you are learning to write these kinds of questions.

I have devoted a whole chapter to multiple-choice questions that tap higher-order thinking because I believe they are an underused resource and because they can be fun to construct and to use with students. They are a useful alternative to writing-intensive questions, either when you want students to think about more problems in a shorter time than they could if they had to write answers or when you want to assess the higher-order thinking of students for whom writing is a particular challenge. In addition, multiple-choice questions don't take much time to score, so it's easy to give students feedback in a timely fashion.

We turn now to open-ended questions (Chapter 5) and performance assessments (Chapters 6 through 8), which also elicit evidence of students' thinking but often do involve writing skills.

5 Open-Ended Questions

Questions are so much more than sentences that happen to end with question marks. Questions are an invitation to respond, and what you ask in a question will make a huge difference in the nature of the response. There are many ways to describe question-asking, but for the purposes of this book—eliciting higher-order thinking in students' responses—I discuss in this chapter the difference between *open* and *closed* questions.

Open and Closed Questions

In a nutshell, *closed* questions have one right answer or one correct solution set, and *open* questions have multiple good answers or several different solutions. "What is the capital of Montana?" is a closed question. "Why might someone want to live in Helena, Montana?" is an open question.

Closed questions usually require thinking at the Remember, Understand, or Apply level, as in these examples:

- What number comes after 7? (Remember)
- What is a prime number? (Understand)
- What is 375 divided by 15? (Apply)

Identifying exactly what knowledge and skills these closed questions require of students is fairly straightforward. In the first question, students have to *remember* that 8 comes after 7 when they count. In the second question, students have to *understand* what a prime number is in order to be able to give their own definition or description. In the third question, students have to *apply* an algorithm that they have learned in order to divide. Some students may apply different algorithms, but any algorithm that properly solves the problem will be mathematically equivalent and return the answer 25.

Open questions usually require thinking at the Analyze, Evaluate, or Create level, as in the following examples:

- Describe three different ways to calculate $-3/2 \times 2/5$. (Analyze)
- You are solving a problem that asks you to figure out how far a truck driver will drive in 3.5 hours. Would it be more helpful to you to know how many miles he drives in an hour or how many miles he drives in 15 minutes? Why? (Evaluate)
- Write a word problem that you can use $15 \div 3$ to solve. (Create)

Notice that these open-ended questions call for content knowledge (mathematics, in this case). They align with the Common Core mathematics standards' domains (including Operations and Algebraic Thinking, Numbers and Operations, and so on) and practices (including reasoning and problem solving). You could also ask open-ended questions in cases where content knowledge is less important—for example, "What is your favorite number?" In this chapter, we'll concentrate on open-ended questions that make student thinking about content visible.

One important thing to notice about these open questions is that they are more difficult to write well, and take more time and thought on your part, than closed questions. It is, therefore, very important to plan these questions ahead of time. You may not be able to come up with on-the-fly open questions that have students thinking about content in the way you intend.

The second important aspect to notice is that you have to think carefully about exactly what knowledge and skills these open questions require, more so than for closed questions. For the Analyze example, students need a range of content knowledge. They need to know there is more than one way to solve a problem, they need to know something about multiplying fractions and about negative numbers, and they need to know some general ways in which number sentences can be manipulated. Depending on the specific solutions students give, they also need to know something about proportions, decimals, fractions, and mixed numbers. Regarding thinking skills, students need to analyze the requirements of the problem and match those to three different solution strategies. As for the multiple-choice questions in Chapter 4, analyzing the questions from the perspective of solving the problem the question asks allows you to see whether the question matches an intended learning standard—in this case, solving problems that require the multiplication of fractions, negative numbers, and mathematical reasoning.

To answer the Evaluate question, students need content knowledge about solving time-and-distance problems, about multiplying decimals, and about units of measure. Regarding thinking skills, students need to analyze the requirements of the problem using 15 minutes as the unit of measure and using hours as the unit of measure; evaluate these two options for speed, efficiency, or personal preference; and then select and defend the choice that makes sense based on this evaluation.

For the Create question, students need content knowledge about the purpose of division—the sorts of problems and situations for which division is useful. Regarding thinking skills, they need to create a scenario for a word problem that is an instance of that kind of problem or situation. The Common Core mathematics standards for both content and practice are in play for all of these questions.

A third important point to recognize is that students need more time to answer open questions than closed questions. Make sure to allow plenty of wait time. It may help to develop routines that help students see they're not just "waiting" but are actively processing. One simple strategy is just to call their attention to the fact that waiting to answer will help with responding ("Take your time to think about this"). A second strategy is "no hands up," where you designate a certain amount of time for thinking and then call on students, either with hand-raising or by using a random calling strategy, only after they have all had some time to think. A third strategy for extending wait time and making sure all students have something to say is think-pair-share. Students get some time to think of their own answers and then turn to a partner and share their answers, so by the time you call on someone to speak to the whole group, everyone has at least two possible ideas (their own and their partner's) and has had some time to think about both of them.

The set of mathematics examples presented earlier supports the argument that open questions give evidence about both *what* students know and *how they think about* what they know. Although both closed and open questions can give evidence of what facts and concepts students know, only open questions give evidence about what students can do with that knowledge. I also hope this little set of examples shows how careful you have to be when preparing open questions to make sure both the content and the thinking skills students use match directly with the standards, curricular goals, and thinking skills you are trying to help them learn.

Writing Open Questions

To invite student thinking, especially divergent thinking, you must craft your open questions carefully, because *you will get what you ask for.* Write questions that intentionally and obviously have more than one good answer. Remember, the existence of multiple good answers doesn't mean "anything goes"; there will, of course, be many ways to answer open questions with a sketchy response or just plain erroneously. And questions will vary in degree of openness, amount of scaffolding, and acceptance of alternative responses.

What follow are some suggestions on how to write open questions. Please remember to analyze your question before using it to make sure that what it asks students to think about aligns with the content and thinking skills you intend to teach and assess. That is the most important criterion for your open question, not whether it follows any particular writing suggestion.

Open Questions in Mathematics

I once had a workshop participant ask me how open questions applied in mathematics, because, as she said, "Mathematics is so cut and dried." Oh, dear! Mathematics is *not* cut and dried unless it's taught that way. Mathematics is based on understanding and interpreting patterns. It just begs for open questions—at least, it does if students are going to learn to think like mathematicians instead of like calculators.

The suggestions I offer here for creating open questions in mathematics come from Small's (2012) wonderful book, *Good Questions: Great Ways to Differentiate*

Mathematics Instruction. The explanations and examples are mine, and any errors or omissions are mine as well. If you want more information about questions in mathematics, I recommend Small's book.

One way to write open questions in mathematics is to *turn a closed question around* and, at the same time, open up at least one of the parameters in the question so that more than one answer is possible (Small, 2012). For example, consider the closed question "What is one-third of 36?" If you just turn the question around, it's still closed: "12 is what fraction of 36?" But if you turn it around and open it up just a bit, you have an open question: "12 is a fraction of a number. What could the fraction and number be?"

Another way to write open questions in mathematics is to *ask for similarities and differences between two mathematical items* (Small, 2012). The items could be numbers, graphs, shapes, measurements, proportions, even math problems. So, for example, if you're studying numbers in 1st grade, you might ask, "How is the number 15 like the number 20, and how is it different?" There are many interesting answers to that question that relate directly to important learning outcomes in numbers and operations. Or, if you're studying linear functions in 8th grade, you might ask, "How are these two graphs alike, and how are they different?" (see Figure 5.1).

Figure 5.1 Graph Comparison

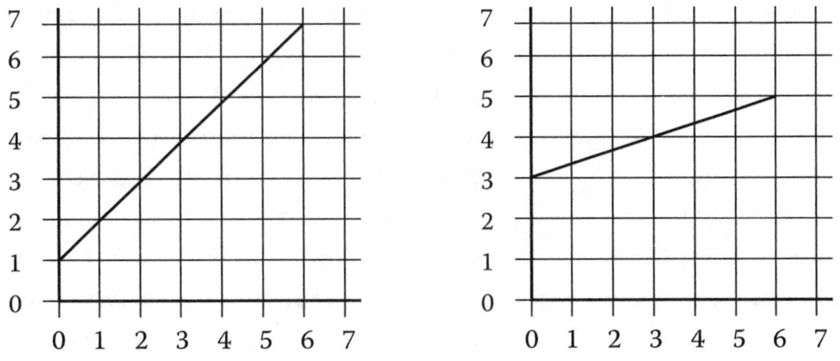

Again, there are many interesting answers to that question that relate directly to important learning outcomes in the study of functions.

A third way Small (2012) suggests you can create open questions in mathematics is to *replace a number with a blank*. Let students choose the numbers and then use them to solve the problem. For example, a closed question might be "Darnice baked cookies for herself and her sister to take to their classes at school. She baked 3 dozen cookies and gave 16 of them to her sister. How many cookies does Darnice have to take to her class?" An open version of that might be "She baked __ dozen cookies and gave __ of them to her sister. . . ."

A fourth way Small (2012) suggests you can create open questions in mathematics is to ask students to *create a sentence that includes words and numbers that you specify*. For example, you might say, "Write a sentence that uses the numbers 3 and 5 as well as the words *greater* and *less*." Students could write a variety of such sentences (e.g., "3 and 5 are greater than 2 but less than 7"; "3 is less than 5 and greater than 1"; "3 times 5 is greater than 10 and less than 20"), all of which would give evidence of student thinking directly related to mathematical content and practices in numbers and operations.

A fifth strategy from Small (2012) is to *use words that are somewhat indefinite*. This approach opens up an infinite number of solutions and requires students to explain how their solution fits the problem. For example, instead of the closed question "Draw two rectangles with the same area," you might say, "Draw two rectangles with areas that are different but close" and then ask students to explain their thinking.

A sixth strategy Small (2012) suggests is that *some questions can be changed from closed to open by revising them*. This is a good strategy to use if you find that problem after problem in a text or other resource is a closed question. For example, "George's farm has chickens and pigs. George sees 9 animals and 26 legs in the barnyard. How many chickens and how many pigs are there?" This problem can be revised to admit multiple solutions, although this version still is closed because there is a finite solution set: "George's farm has chickens and pigs. George sees 26 legs in the barnyard. How many chickens and how many pigs could there be?" It can be made more open by further revision: "George's farm has chickens and pigs. Help George write a story about his barnyard by deciding how many chickens and how many pigs there might be. With that many chickens and pigs, how many legs would there be?" Although technically this is still a closed question, because it has a solution set that can be described mathematically, it's still much more open than the original.

Interpreting Information in English and in Content Areas

The questions in the right-hand column of the idea bank in Figure 4.1 (p. 39) include many examples that work for constructing open questions as well as multiple-choice questions. Notice that these suggestions are about the content of the question to be asked (e.g., "What is the most credible piece of evidence that...?"). I won't repeat these content suggestions here. Rather, I'll use this section to suggest some ways to approach the actual writing of the questions.

I always *start with a direct approach.* Simply ask students to analyze, evaluate, or create material appropriate to the content and thinking skills you want to assess. Here are some examples asking students to think about the Preamble to the U.S. Constitution.

> We the people of the United States, in order to form a more perfect union, establish justice, insure domestic tranquility, provide for the common defense, promote the general welfare, and secure the blessings of liberty to ourselves and our posterity, do ordain and establish this Constitution for the United States of America.

- The Preamble to the Constitution lists purposes or reasons for creating the Constitution. Those purposes assume that a "good society" has certain characteristics. What are these assumptions? (Analyze)
- Which of the purposes listed in the Preamble do you think will turn out to be the most difficult purpose for the newly formed United States to fulfill? Explain your thinking. (Evaluate)
- Suppose that in a fictional society, all of the purposes in the Preamble were perfectly fulfilled all the time. What would that society look like? (Create)

I have included the level of thinking for each example in the list. Analyzing these questions according to what problem the student has to solve leads to the conclusion that each question assesses something slightly different. In addition to different thinking skills, each question assesses slightly different content knowledge. All of the questions require comprehension of the Preamble. The first example also assesses some understanding of the nature of government and possibly theories of government. The second example also assesses some understanding of U.S. history. The third example is less about comprehension of the realities of government and history and more about logical extension of the purposes in the Preamble, and perhaps some understanding of the concept of a utopia.

A simple, direct question is often the clearest statement of what you want to ask. However, the following paragraphs describe some rhetorical devices you can use if a direct question seems strained, awkward, or lacking in context. You may recognize these strategies, because we also used them to write multiple-choice questions in Chapter 4. Remember that these suggestions are about *how* to write the questions, not *what* to write. For the content of the questions, use the categories in Figure 4.1.

Another way to write an open question is to *describe a fictional student.* That way, you can create more and less acceptable or complete points of view, harmlessly attribute them to someone who does not exist, and help students concentrate on the point of view itself and not the author. Let's first look at the following example.

> Two students disagreed about whether air is a natural resource. Brianna said it is, because it is a material found in nature that is useful to people. Tony said it isn't, because air isn't a material that you can collect or move around; you just use the air around you. Can you think of any more arguments for Brianna's or Tony's point of view?

Using the "what problem to solve" analysis, it seems that this question requires student thinking at the Analyze level regarding understanding of natural resources and their use and management. Students' responses to the question would make visible their understanding of this content and their ability to reason logically with this understanding.

You can use the opinions of real students to help frame follow-up questions, as long as the tenor of the question does not involve showing someone up as right or wrong. For example, in a class discussion on floating and sinking, two students might have disagreed. You could then say, "Aisha thinks the wooden ball will float and the rubber ball will sink. Drew thinks they both will sink. How can we figure out whether one of them is correct?" Using the "what problem to solve" analysis, this question requires students to create or design a demonstration that will allow them to conclude whether the balls sink or float. Content knowledge about experimental design is required, but in the question as written, an understanding of sinking and floating—including the concepts of mass, volume, and relative density—is *not* required. A teacher who used this question and who wanted to hear students' explanations and understanding of mass, volume, and relative density would have to frame an additional question asking about the reasons for the sinking or floating results. Be careful, then, not to confuse the *topic* of a question with the content knowledge and skills it assesses. The way to figure out what exactly a question assesses is to use our "what problem to solve" analysis or something equivalent.

If a question needs context in order to make sense, *set up a scenario* as you write your open question. We use scenarios in mathematics word problems all the time, but we don't always think to use them to set up problems in other disciplines. For example, look at the following scenario.

> You just moved into a new house, and you want to plant a vegetable garden in the backyard. However, the backyard is on a pretty steep hill. How might you design your vegetable garden to protect it from the effects of erosion?

Analyzing this question from the point of view of what problem the student would have to solve to answer it, you can see that this question requires thinking at the Create level (designing a garden). It also requires some content knowledge about growing plants, water erosion, and, to a lesser extent, wind erosion of soil.

Overall, then, we can identify some general principles to summarize how to write open questions about the interpretation of information in English and the content areas. First, specify the content (whether it's information from text or understanding of some concepts, or both) and thinking skills you want to assess. Next, write a question that asks students to analyze, evaluate, or create (depending on the thinking skill desired) the appropriate material. Use Figure 4.1 to help select the kind of material and question you will use, based on the kind of thinking you want to assess. You can either ask the question directly or set it in a scenario about a fictional student or in a scenario that gives a reasonable context for the question.

Open Questions in Science

We have already used some science examples in the previous section. Science, like mathematics, is a discipline that just begs for using open-ended questions to develop particular thinking skills, but again, like mathematics, it can be taught merely as a collection of facts to learn. To help educators teach science in a way that helps students develop scientific thinking skills, the National Research Council produced a book called *Ready, Set, Science! Putting Research to Work in K–8 Science Classrooms* (Michaels, Shouse, & Schweingruber, 2007). This book includes an entire chapter on making student thinking visible by using talk and argument. Reading that chapter, one is struck by the similarities between the effective classroom "talk moves" (p. 90) described for science and the questioning moves described for formative assessment and furthering student learning in any discipline (Brown & Wragg, 1993; Moss & Brookhart, 2009).

Although the principle that students learn through talk and argument is a general one across many disciplines, learning to talk in the language of science is a discipline-related skill (Michaels et al., 2007). Similarly, there is a discipline-related aspect to argument in science, because the logic and the empirical support for scientific arguments need to be based in scientific interpretations as opposed to unscientific interpretations. Within those disciplinary boundaries, however, Michaels and her colleagues recommend classroom discussion based on open questions of the sort described earlier, with follow-up questions designed to help students listen to one another, process one another's arguments, and further the discussion. The authors recommend six talk moves, or strategies (p. 91), which, with the exception of using wait time, can also be strategies for asking open questions:

- Ask students to agree or disagree as you restate their reasoning in other words, which the authors call "revoicing"; for example, "So let me see if I understand what you are saying. You're thinking the ball will roll faster as it goes downhill because the force of gravity will be greater than the rolling resistance."
- Ask students to restate someone else's reasoning; for example, "Bruno, can you tell us what Ashleigh just said using your own words?"
- Ask students to apply their own reasoning to the argument of another; for example, "Tuyen, do you agree or disagree with Lucas's explanation of why the tides were so high yesterday?"
- Ask students to further the discussion by adding to it; for example, "Does anyone have anything to add?"
- Ask students to explain their reasoning; for example, "How do you know?" or "What evidence helps support your conclusion?"
- Use wait time.

These strategies work to further scientific thinking. They are also applicable more broadly, using concepts, terminology, and arguments from other disciplines. The point I hope this section has made is that there are some general strategies that you can use to write open questions (e.g., turn a question around, cite a fictional student), but to be *useful for learning*, any of these strategies needs to be situated in a content area. Open questions that are not thus situated (e.g., "What would you like for your birthday?") may be interesting, but they do not assess learning and thinking in a content area.

Using Open Questions

Brief, open-ended questions of the sort described in this chapter are useful for many purposes. Here I discuss three such purposes: oral classroom discussion questions, exit tickets and other formative assessment strategies, and essay test questions.

Oral Questions for Class Discussion

Open-ended questions support classroom discussion better than closed questions do. When a student responds to an open question, rather than replying yourself, ask another student to get involved: "What is Cole telling us? What can you add that will help us think about this?" In addition to furthering students' thinking, this approach helps students learn to listen to one another (Moss & Brookhart, 2009).

My personal favorite example of this is the rhetorical question at the end of *The Cat in the Hat* (Dr. Seuss, 1957). After an afternoon of mayhem caused by an energetic cat who attempts to entertain Sally and her brother while their mother is out, the cat manages to clean up and make his escape before Mother gets home. Mother asks the children what they did while she was out, but they do not answer. The book ends with the question, "What would you do if your mother asked you?" This is possibly the first open question I remember from my own school days!

It would also be a great question to start a class discussion. As written, the question elicits thinking at the Create level and asks students to make connections with their own lives. What one child might do could differ from what another might do, depending on personality and situation. Follow-up questions could ask students to restate one another's reasoning, to agree or disagree with it, and to imagine what Mother's response might be to the various answers. In addition to the thinking skills, students would need content knowledge about the plot and characters in the book and about their own lives (and mothers).

Teachers who wanted to center the discussion more on the plot and characters of the book could ask students to answer from the point of view of Sally or her brother; for example, "What do you think Sally should do? Why?" Again, follow-up questions could ask students to examine one another's reasoning, support or refute that reasoning with evidence from the book, envision consequences, and so on. In addition to thinking skills, students would need content knowledge about the plot and characters in the book and would need to understand at least a little bit about the concept of author's purpose. The book is a fantasy, but it also was a bit of a polemic against "ordinary" children's books, and the outrageousness of the cat and what he was trying to do for the children could become part of the discussion of what the children should do.

Almost all of the other examples of open questions in this chapter could be used in oral classroom discussion. The key for any of them is to open the floor to many different points of view, ask for reasoning and evidence, and listen to what the responses tell you about student thinking and understanding. Another excellent strategy to advance class discussions is to teach students how to ask their own open-ended questions. You can read more about that in Moss and Brookhart (2009).

Exit Tickets and Other Formative Assessment Strategies

When you think about it, many formative assessment strategies are really a format, and their effectiveness depends on the questions with which they are used. Exit tickets, whiteboards, thumbs up/down, and a host of other similar strategies are ways for students to respond to make their thinking explicit. How much and what kind of evidence of learning that thinking shows depend entirely on the quality of the question you ask and how well that question matches learning intentions.

For example, consider a 6th grade science classroom where students have finished a series of lessons identifying and describing natural resources and distinguishing renewable from nonrenewable resources. The teacher's learning goals for the lessons were that students understand what natural resources are, know where they may be found, and can describe some ways they may be managed. Before going on to the rest of the unit, the teacher wants to use an exit ticket to find out how students understand what a natural resource is. Consider what students would write if the exit ticket prompt was "What is a natural resource?" This is a closed question that requires thinking at the Remember or Understand level. Most of the students would probably write the definition from their science textbook or from class discussion, either as memorized (Remember) or in their own words (Understand).

Now consider what information students and teachers would get if the exit ticket prompt was an open question. There are several possibilities; the teacher would probably use only one. I list just two here as examples:

- Look around the classroom. Name at least five different natural resources in use and explain where they came from. Are any of these nonrenewable resources? (Analyze)

- What do you think is the most important natural resource in [name of the school's state or region]? Why do you think so? (Evaluate)

To answer these questions, students would need the content knowledge that the teacher has in mind (understanding natural resources). The students would also have to *use* that knowledge (at the Analyze or Evaluate level). Therefore, the students' responses to either of these exit ticket prompts would allow both teacher and students to see how students could bring what they know about natural resources to bear on a "problem" (in the sense we used that word in Chapter 2). Teacher and students would have evidence of the degree to which students could put their understanding of natural resources to work.

Exit tickets are not the only formative assessment strategy that works well with open questions, although in my view they are particularly well suited for doing so. For any formative assessment strategy that is based on a question, using an open as opposed to a closed question will give insight into student thinking as well as content knowledge.

We have just considered the important role that open questions play in formative assessment. In my experience, it's more common to hear people talk about using open questions in formative assessment than in summative assessment. However, it's critically important to align the kinds of thinking your summative assessments require with the kinds of thinking your formative assessment requires—and, ultimately, both of these should align with the learning goals you and your students are aiming for.

Essay Test Questions

One of the biggest missed opportunities in the use of questions is in essay test questions. So many are just recall questions dressed up to seem like essays—for example, "List and describe all the steps in the life cycle of a butterfly." That is a closed question at the Remember level. If all you want to know is whether the student has memorized the steps in the life cycle of a butterfly, multiple-choice or fill-in-the-blank questions are a much more efficient use of testing time. What essay questions are really good for is allowing students to show you how they can use what they know.

Consider a science or geography class that is studying the effects of resources on life in different parts of the world. An essay test question that is open allows you much more of a window into student understanding and thinking than one that is closed. Consider the following examples.

> *Poor example, closed question:* Name an area of the world that has a severe hunger problem, and list its causes.
>
> *Good example, open question:* List two factors that contribute to hunger in a developing country. Choose one of these factors and discuss a long-term solution for it. The discussion should include both an advantage and a disadvantage of this solution.
>
> National Assessment of Educational Progress (NAEP) released items: 2005, grade 12, block S13, question #13.

In the poor example, students are asked to recall some facts they learned in class. At best, the question assesses thinking at the Understand level, if students put the explanations they have already learned into their own words. Think about the problem students must solve in order to answer the question in the good example. They need to think at the Create level (designing a long-term solution) and base their creation on knowledge and understanding about the causes of hunger, regional climate systems, and the geography (and perhaps politics) involved in moving or developing food resources. So the content is covered, but the students also need to use their content knowledge. You would assess the answers to this essay question not so much according to the brilliance of the students' solution to the problem of world hunger, but in terms of the content and reasoning supporting their argument for the solution they proposed.

A Key to Improved Student Learning

If you could remember only one thing from this entire book, I would hope it would be how to write open questions. If you could develop only one disposition after reading this entire book, I would hope it would be to believe that using more, and more carefully constructed, open questions is an important key to improving student learning. If helping students think and getting evidence of student thinking are significant goals for you, it follows that open questions are *that* important. Students can't answer what you don't ask.

Using open questions helps teach students some lessons about learning as well as thinking about content. Open questions help students learn to listen to one another. Open questions help students dispel the naïve notion that knowledge is fixed, that teachers "own" it, and that learning means delivering back to teachers a set of facts students were responsible for memorizing. Many students hold this "theory" of what knowledge is (Schommer, Calvert, Gariglietti, & Bajaj, 1997). Until students realize that learning is more of a quest for answers to important questions than a series of quizzes to pass, they will not be able to reach any pinnacle of understanding.

In this chapter, I have defined open questions and described how to write open questions in different disciplines. We looked at how to use open questions for class discussion, exit tickets and other formative assessment strategies, and essay test questions. Finally, I exhorted you to use open questions as much as possible in order to stretch your students' thinking and to give you evidence of what that thinking looks like. Questions are invitations for students to respond, and open questions help make sure those responses are deep, thoughtful interactions with the content students are learning.

6 Performance Assessment Tasks: The Basics

Performance assessments require students to do something—to create a product, to perform a process, or both. As you read in Chapter 3, performance assessments have two parts: (1) the performance task and (2) the criteria and scoring scheme by which the performance will be evaluated. A performance task without a scoring scheme that maps the student performance with fidelity back to the knowledge and skills you intended to assess is not a performance assessment, it's just an activity. In this book, I concentrate on how to design and write the performance task, and I focus on performance tasks that assess higher-order thinking and require judgment-based scoring.

When a standard requires students to carry out some activity (e.g., use an electronic card catalog, play a clarinet part, prepare a slide for viewing, dribble a basketball), performance assessment tasks that ask students to demonstrate skills or processes are useful. When a standard requires students to use knowledge and skills they have acquired to create some sort of product (e.g., a bookcase, a model of a plant cell, an original short story, an essay on Shakespeare's treatment of gender roles in his sonnets, a report on the use of performance-enhancing drugs in professional sports), performance assessment tasks that ask students to create a product are useful.

Sometimes performance tasks require higher-order thinking, and sometimes they don't. This chapter will concentrate on those that do. For example, knowing the parts of an entry in an electronic card catalog reflects simple content knowledge; using an electronic card catalog effectively to obtain certain resources for a particular purpose requires higher-order thinking. Dribbling a basketball in a drill reflects psychomotor skills; dribbling a basketball flexibly (moving slower and faster, with bigger and smaller steps) in a game to avoid opponents' moves and blocks and to get past the opponents and into a position to score requires higher-order thinking as well.

Basic Guidelines for Creating Performance Assessment Tasks

The first step in creating any assessment is to identify the learning outcomes you want to assess. Performance assessments are no different. The following steps present a convenient way to think about the design process for performance assessments:

1. Identify the *content knowledge and skills* to be assessed.
2. Identify the *thinking skills* to be assessed.
3. Draft a task and criteria to match these intended learning outcomes.
4. Check your draft to evaluate the match with intended content and thinking skills.
5. Check that the requirements of the task don't add additional, irrelevant skills.
6. Revise the task, and develop the criteria into rubrics by adding descriptions of performance levels.
7. Try out the task and the rubrics. Revise as necessary.

Drafting a task includes writing complete directions for students, but that doesn't mean specifying everything and doing students' thinking for them. Typically, directions for performance assessments will include a description of the problem, question, or task; a description of the strategies and materials students will use to solve the problem, answer the question, or do the task; and a description of the requirements for the solution, answer, performance, or final product. Chapter 7 describes how you can vary the amount of scaffolding in each of these to leave more or less room for student choice. The more students have to do on their own, the more opportunities they have for higher-order thinking and the more varied their performances will be. The more you specify what students have to do, the fewer opportunities students will have for higher-order thinking and the more similar their performances will be to one another.

Consider this example. A high school history teacher wants to create a performance assessment that will help his students both consolidate and extend knowledge of the 20th century events they have been studying and use this knowledge to inform their growing understanding of some big ideas in history. To do this, he decides to ask his students to compare and contrast two stories or "texts," both of which they have studied: World War I and World War II.

First, he identifies the *content knowledge and skills to be assessed*: knowledge of facts and concepts about World Wars I and II; understanding of historical perspective; and understanding of the effects of power, technology, and geography on human events (and wars in particular).

Second, he identifies the *thinking skills* he wants to assess. Specifically, he wants students to be able to identify various aspects of the two world wars, use comparison and contrast to determine how these aspects were alike and different, and then reason by induction to draw conclusions about larger themes—such as balance of power and the effects of technology and geography—from these comparisons. This is thinking at the Analyze level of Bloom's taxonomy. This is also thinking that requires using logic to construct an argument and support it with details about the wars and their similarities and differences.

Third, he drafts a task and criteria. He decides that simply asking a question such as "How are World War I and World War II alike and different?" is too broad. Yet he decides that making a comparison chart for students to fill in (e.g., time periods, causes, countries involved, weaponry, casualties, locations of battles, outcomes, aftermath) would result in too narrow a task and would not require the higher-order thinking he wants students to do. His first draft of the task goes like this.

It is said that those who cannot remember the past are condemned to repeat it. Do you think 21st century citizens can learn anything from the major wars of the 20th century?

- Create a report addressing the question "How are World War I and World War II alike and different? What can we learn from these similarities and differences?"
- You can use any method you like to gather and organize your information. You may use written and electronic sources. You may use a chart or other visual organizer to help present the information you gather.
- Your final report should include a section describing what you did to gather information to address the question, a section comparing and contrasting aspects of the two wars, and a section drawing conclusions about what we in the 21st century can learn from these similarities and differences.

Your report will be assessed according to the following criteria: (1) accuracy and completeness of information about the wars for the purposes of comparison; (2) logic and clarity of explanation of the similarities and differences you describe; (3) quality of your conclusions.

The teacher's fourth step is to check the task's draft to evaluate how well it aligns with intended standards with regard to both content and thinking skills. He finds that the match between the task and the intended learning outcomes is pretty good. However, he wonders if students will draw conclusions in the three broad areas—balance of power, the effects of new technologies (especially new weaponry), and geography—he has in mind, because there is nothing in the task or criteria that would prompt them to do so. If students don't go for these "big ideas," he wouldn't know why or why not—whether students were unable to do so or simply didn't interpret the assignment in the way he intended. Therefore, he decides to edit the last part of the last bullet to read "… and a section drawing conclusions about what we in the 21st century can learn about big concepts in history (e.g., power, technology, geography) from these similarities and differences." He also edits the third assessment criterion to read "quality of your conclusions about big concepts in history (e.g., power, technology, geography)."

Fifth, the teacher checks that the requirements of the task don't add additional, irrelevant skills. In addition to the learning standards he has identified, he realizes students would need research and reading skills to accomplish this task. These skills are relevant to studying history but are not specifically the learning outcomes the assignment is intended to tap. Therefore, he decides to provide additional scaffolding in the research process for a few students and to make sure that appropriate material is available at a variety of reading levels. Having thus revised the task, his next steps are to develop the criteria into rubrics by adding descriptions of performance levels, and to try out the task and rubrics.

Varying and Controlling Features of Performance Assessment Tasks

Varying and controlling different features of performance assessment tasks will help you design tasks that measure exactly the learning outcomes you intend to measure. In general, the more open and complex a task is, and the more time it takes, the more the student will have to use higher-order thinking. This doesn't mean I am arguing for every assignment to be long, complex, and unstructured. What is important is that you recognize the effects that various features of tasks have on the learning that is assessed, and vary them intentionally to design the task that you want.

For example, if you want to know that your students can count by 5s, you should simply ask them to do that. The sequence of numbers they say or write will be correct or incorrect. All students who do this well will give the same answer. However, if you want to know how students interpret patterns in numbers and how they can use their number sense to solve problems, you can ask them to invent problems for which counting by 5s might be a useful strategy and to explain their thinking. Students who do this well will give a variety of different answers and explanations. Some might write problems about time on an analog clock, some might write problems about nickels and dimes, some might write problems about football yard lines, and so on.

Performance assessments vary in many ways. In this book, I emphasize five of these variables: task length, group or individual work, amount of task structure, cognitive level, and difficulty level. The next two sections discuss task length and using group or individual work. These are fairly straightforward decisions to make when you are designing performance assessment tasks. Chapter 7 discusses varying and controlling the amount of task structure. Chapter 8 discusses varying and controlling the cognitive level and the difficulty of the tasks you design. I have put these last two in the same chapter in order to clearly distinguish between them and—I hope—dispel the myth that cognitive level and difficulty level are the same thing. They are not.

Varying and Controlling Task Length

Long-term projects usually assess several standards and several thinking skills, and they may include mixed response modes. For example, a term paper may require writing a research question, doing library work to gather information, reading and analyzing the information to answer the question, and preparing a written paper. Sometimes an assignment to do a written report also requires making an oral presentation to the class. A science assignment may require designing and conducting an experiment, and then writing a lab report or constructing a science fair presentation. An assignment in several disciplines may involve making a model of a piece of equipment (a camera), a structure (an atom, a solar system), or an event (a Civil War battle), plus writing an explanation. Some of the complexity of an assignment is related to the number of "pieces" it contains.

As the complexity of a task increases, its potential multiplies—but so do its risks. A poorly designed long-term project that amounts to little more than gathering and reproducing resources on a topic (e.g., a PowerPoint presentation of facts about elements and compounds copied from the Internet) has greater potential for harm than a poorly designed open-ended question, because it wastes so much more learning time.

The following is an example I love to hate! It is a good example of how making a task more complex "just for the fun of it" (or for whatever reason) leads to an assessment that does not match intended standards and can really do harm.

***Wanted:* Explorer**

We have been studying explorers. Now it is your turn to be an explorer. Design and draw your sailing vessel. Chart your voyage on the map. Include a compass rose, a map key, and a map scale. Complete a trip log (journal) to record the events of your voyage. Write a report about your adventures. Tell why you decided to go on your voyage, what you took with you, what you expected to find, and what you actually found. Be descriptive, creative, and imaginative. The final report can be typed, printed, or written in cursive (use ink). Your report should include the following:

- Cover page
- Title page (title, date, name)
- Written report (four paragraphs minimum)
- Drawing of your vessel
- Map of your voyage
- Trip log

This is a long assignment. It has many parts, and it requires that students use several different media (drawings, maps, writing) to communicate. However, it doesn't take long to figure out that this performance assessment does *not* match intended standards about understanding the human impetus for exploration; the effects of politics, trade, technology, and geography on exploration; or even knowing facts about explorers. Rather, this task, at best, assesses map skills and creative writing. One (admittedly smart-aleck) teacher in a workshop said to me, "I'd draw an oval and tell the teacher that it was my pod and I was going to explore the moon."

Sometimes a good counterexample helps make a point, and I hope that's what this example did. Just adding time and complexity to an assignment does *not* mean that you are adding higher-order thinking to it. In fact, you are adding opportunities for extraneous skills (in this case, drawing and creative writing) to creep in and distort the assessment information you glean from student performance.

Varying and Controlling Amount of Group Work

Should students do their work individually or in groups? That depends in large part on the knowledge and skills you intend to assess. I recommend that, whether you use group work or not, you assess what *individuals* learned (Brookhart, 2013a). The reason for this recommendation is that you are obligated to teach each student. Formative assessment that will help each student know what he or she needs to learn next requires individual information about learning, as does summative assessment that will report accurately to each student and the student's parents how well important curricular objectives and standards have been attained. You can collect information at the group level for attributes of the group itself, such as collaboration, organization, and cooperation.

These principles have implications for how you integrate group work into your performance assessments. In many cases, groups working together can function efficiently to do tasks that all students need to do. For example, if an assessment requires that a number of observations be made and recorded, over time, about the growth of algae in five different jars in order to test a hypothesis about the effects of various contaminants, students can do that in groups. Otherwise, you would have 125 jars in a class of 25 students! However, to find out what each student learned from analyzing those observations, you need information from each student. There are other types of tasks where you could assign either group or individual work—for example, doing a research project on a historical, scientific, or literary figure. On the one hand, students may enjoy working together, and they would be able to share strategies and resources if they work in groups. On the other hand, individual work makes it easier for you to assess what an individual student knows and can do. How should you proceed?

First, decide whether you want the students to work together or not, given your knowledge of the content, your curriculum, and the needs of your students. Then, if you have decided to involve students in some group work, decide how you will assess individual learning. There are many ways to have students work and learn together, and then to find out via individual assessments what each student learned. I suggest using one of following five strategies, depending on the nature of the performance assessment (Brookhart, 2013a).

Student reflection on learning. For simple group projects, students can do the project and then write (or speak, in some cases) a reflection on what they learned from the project. The key to the success of this strategy is the quality of your reflection prompt. "Summarize what you learned" is too broad. Design a reflection prompt that will make students actually use what they learned. Consider the following example.

> You've examined the history of the NASA space launches and the role of astronauts in space exploration. Summarize the role of astronauts from the start of the space program until today, and predict what the role of astronauts will be in the future as technology becomes more advanced.

Oral questioning. When you assign an oral presentation to groups and when each group will present something different—as, for example, when each group specializes in a family of elements from the periodic table and makes a presentation to teach the class about "their family of elements"—you can build time for oral questioning into the presentation. You should prepare these questions ahead of time, and they should reflect intentions for student learning. For example, you might ask, "How do the electrons in each of your elements determine the characteristics of the elements?"—not "Tell me about your element." Pose these questions to individual students and assess the degree to which they can articulate what they have learned.

Multistep design. Probably the most effective way to incorporate individual assessment into group projects is to design multiple opportunities for formative assessment as the project is being completed, so individuals can receive feedback on their learning progress, and then have one or more summative assessments as the obvious ultimate follow-up to those formative assessments. For example, students can submit brief reflections after they have worked on writing a research question, creating a hypothesis, or devising a project plan. You can give feedback to students individually on the quality of their initial understanding of the topic and intended learning. You can have students write brief paragraphs at various checkpoints during the completion of the project, giving feedback to individuals again about what they are learning. You might also build in a formative assessment at the group level about the group process. Finally, after the project is complete, you can have students repeat one of the small individual assignments and couple your assessment of their work with evidence from what they accomplished in the group to evaluate the individual's learning from the project.

"Write your own questions." For performance assessments that lend themselves to understanding questions in a discipline—either math or science problems or questions about history or literature, for example—you can ask students at various points during the completion of a group project to write individual questions of the type that they are learning to solve (and, of course, to solve them). Then, after the group project is complete, you can have students solve another problem of this type. Combine this individual assessment with evidence of what they accomplished in the group to evaluate each student's learning.

Post-project test. Finally, some group projects are really instructional activities, not performance assessments. For example, I once observed a wonderful group project where each group "acted out" an atom. Students dressed as protons, neutrons, or electrons and stood (or walked, in the case of the electrons) where their atomic particle would be located in a specific element. Rather than grading the "performance" of the group acting out an atom, the teacher used a conventional test later on as the final assessment of what students knew about the structure of atoms.

* * * * * *

This chapter outlined the basic design principles for performance assessment tasks and illustrated them with examples. When you design performance tasks, you make choices about the length of the task, amount of group work, task structure, cognitive level, and difficulty. Each of these choices affects exactly what the task assesses. In effect, these choices become part of your "toolkit" for adjusting your task until it assesses exactly the standard or learning outcome you want to assess. In Chapter 7, we'll discuss controlling the task structure. Chapter 8 finishes this sequence by discussing how to control a task's cognitive level and difficulty.

7 Performance Assessment Tasks: Varying the Amount of Structure

The amount of structure or scaffolding that is built into a task helps determine what kind of thinking students must do to complete the task. Think of the difference between asking a student to paint an original watercolor and providing him with a paint-by-number kit. Both can be interesting tasks, but they serve very different purposes.

This chapter provides a framework for controlling the amount of structure or scaffolding in performance assessment tasks. Very structured tasks, like our paint-by-number kit, are not always bad, nor are very unstructured tasks always good. It depends on what you want to assess. The original painting would allow you to see the results of student thinking in matters such as subject selection, composition, use of color, and use of the medium. The paint-by-number task would allow you to observe student skill in using the medium—in this case, watercolors. The key is to have a plan in mind for how you vary the amount of structure you provide for various aspects of the task so that you can control more precisely the thinking skills students must use to do the task.

What Does *Task Structure* Mean, and How Can You Control It?

I use the term *task structure* to mean the amount of scaffolding you provide for each aspect of the task. Task structure in performance assessment is roughly analogous to the open/closed distinction for questions. I like the term *structure* for performance assessments rather than *openness* because tasks usually have many different aspects or elements to them, and in any given task, some elements may be open and some may be closed. Also, the amount of scaffolding possible in various aspects of performance assessment tasks is more a matter of degree; the term *openness* suggests a yes/no decision (open or closed?). But the concept is the same. How much latitude does the student have to make decisions about what to do and how to do it? As we will see, each decision students make allows you a little window into the students' thinking process.

The framework in Figure 7.1 is my own construction, but it is based in research that has been done mostly in the area of science inquiry tasks both at the elementary, middle, and high school levels (BSCS, 2005; Olson & Loucks-Horsley, 2000) and at the college level (Buck, Bretz, & Towns, 2008; Fay, Grove, Towns, & Bretz, 2007). The origin of the work was the need to develop students' scientific thinking. But students don't really learn how to do independent inquiry if their lab manuals are completely structured, like cookbooks. Building on the work of others, these researchers created frameworks that could be used to characterize the level of self-direction, as opposed to teacher direction, in science inquiry projects.

The reason why the framework can be generalized from science inquiry to performance tasks is that questions and tasks, from the students' point of view, are problems to solve. In other words, they require inquiry. Chapter 2 described how that was so, and we have been productively using this approach to analyze the questions and tasks presented as examples in this book and use the results to determine whether the questions and tasks match intended standards. In this chapter, I extend that approach to help us figure out what kinds of thinking we build in to the performance tasks we design. Intentionally controlling task structure is the way to ensure that your task design will require students to do the kind of thinking you want them to do, reflect that thinking in the work, and therefore make that thinking visible and available for assessment. The framework divides tasks into three main features, which I discuss in the following sections.

Figure 7.1 Framework for Controlling the Amount of Structure in Performance Assessment Tasks

	Less Structure ◄		► More Structure
Task Feature	**Not Provided**	**Guided**	**Provided**
Identify problem, pose question, or define task.	Learner poses a question, problem, or task.	Teacher gives learner a selection of questions to choose from or to adapt.	Teacher provides the question, problem, or task.
Select and use strategies and materials for solving problem, answering question, or completing task.	Learner selects strategies and materials.	Teacher suggests strategies and materials for students to use or adapt.	Teacher gives learner strategies and materials.
Present solution, answer, performance, or final product.	Learner decides how to present solution, answer, performance, or final product.	Teacher suggests presentation methods for learner to use or adapt.	Teacher gives learner directions for presentation.

Task Feature #1: Identify the Problem

The first task feature is identifying the problem, posing a question, or defining the task. A performance task always has some sort of question at its root. For example, in the war-related example in Chapter 6 (p. 70), the research questions were "How are World War I and World War II alike and different? What can we learn from these similarities and differences?" Those questions lead to research strategies for finding out the answers and to a final product, a report. A science lab performance assessment might be to design an experiment and find out which brand of cat litter best controls odor. Again, the task is based on a question, which should lead to a hypothesis, an experimental design to test that hypothesis, and a final product in the shape of a lab report. In mathematics, a performance assessment task might be a math problem students need to solve, showing their work and explaining their reasoning. Students will use mathematical strategies and tools to do this, and the final product is the solution and the explanation students write.

OK, you say, it's easy to see that in many research-oriented or mathematics contexts, the framework fits. How about in the arts? What about with creative projects that involve cooking, constructing models, or writing poetry? Actually, the framework fits there, too, because to do any of these things students still must pose for themselves a problem to solve. For example, "How can I paint a painting in the style of Picasso?" or "How can I write a poem that will express my feelings about flowers?" Notice that in addition to setting up problems, each question carries within it the definition of a task (e.g., painting in the style of Picasso). This is the point of this first aspect of performance assessment tasks: students must conceptualize for themselves what the task means and what it entails. This is the "problem" they have to solve.

This feature of performance tasks can be completely structured for students, completely left to students' own discretion, or guided by the teacher in some way. One strategy teachers use to guide students in selecting the problem is to present a list of choices: students can choose, but only from a prepared list. Another is to allow students to adapt the choices in the list: guidance is still provided, but with slightly less structure and slightly more room for student thinking. A strategy with still less structure and even more room for student thinking is to provide one or more criteria for students to use to define their own problem or pose their own question (e.g., a report must be about a real historical event that involved the exercise of First Amendment rights).

Task Feature #2: Strategies and Materials

The second feature of a performance task is selecting and using strategies and materials for solving the problem, answering the question, or completing the task. For science inquiry tasks, this usually means the experimental design and materials. For mathematics problems, this usually means identifying effective solution strategies, carrying them out and evaluating results, and communicating those results to others. For research reports in any discipline, this means determining strategies for locating resources, reading them, and using the information to address the research question. For creating works of art, this means selecting the subject, the medium (acrylics or oils? sonnet or ode?), compositional and expressive strategies (bright colors? imagery about darkness?), and so on. Similarly, for creating "constructions" in any discipline (a diorama of a battle, a model of the solar system, a balsa-wood car that runs on a battery, computer code that runs a web page), this means selecting the strategies, materials, and method to use.

This second element of performance tasks can be completely structured for students, completely left to students' own discretion, or guided by the teacher in some way. The amount of structure in this aspect of the task is not necessarily constrained by the amount of structure the task gave students in identifying the problem or task. For example, you may allow students to choose a painter whose style they will imitate (relatively unstructured), but specify that the students must produce a preliminary drawing on 11-by-17-inch paper, using pencil (very structured).

Sometimes, not only are the strategies left unstructured, but students are also encouraged to come up with *more than one* strategy for solving a problem. For example, you might give students a specific mathematics problem or societal dilemma (very structured) but then ask them to find at least two different ways of solving it.

Task Feature #3: Final Product or Presentation

The third feature of a performance task is presenting the solution, answer, performance, or final product. For performance assessments that result in products, this is the finished work: the report, essay, diorama, or musical composition, for example. Alternatively, some performance assessment tasks assess processes rather than final products, and the third element is the performance in which students demonstrate the process—for example, singing a song.

This third aspect of performance tasks, like the others, can be completely structured for students, completely left to students' own discretion, or guided by the teacher in some way. I have seen a lot of term paper assignments with very detailed directions about the format, length, and outline of the finished report, for example, and I have also seen assignments in which teachers let students make some decisions about how they produce their final work.

Be sure to make a distinction between allowing student choice to encourage interest or provide variety and allowing student choice that gives insight into students' thinking about the content and purpose of the assignment. For example, I once observed a language arts lesson in which the teacher asked students to analyze how a character in a story they had read developed over the course of the narrative; that is, the task definition was very structured. Wanting to add some student choice into the mix, the teacher allowed students to decide among six different methods for their final product. They could write a poem, conduct a presentation with slides, write a song or rap, prepare a brochure, make a poster, or write an essay. Although the method of presenting the final product was guided but still relatively unstructured, that openness didn't really relate to the students' thinking about the character analysis. The choice was independent of the purpose of the assignment itself, based on student preference.

What if the teacher had asked the students to do the character analysis and then present the results in the way they thought the character might? For example, she might have given students choices such as writing a self-reflective letter to another character in the story, or writing a posting for Facebook expressing himself to his friends and followers, or composing a skit consisting of dialogue between the character and another character in the story right after the story ended. Then the choices students made about the final product would also have provided windows into their thinking about the content—in this case, the character.

Let's walk through some examples in several different disciplines, exploring how varying task structure allows you to control the kind of thinking students must do to complete the task.

An Example in Science

The following example is a sample performance assessment intended for use at the upper-elementary or middle school level. This performance assessment addresses several aspects of the Next Generation Science Standards (NRC, 2012), including

- Disciplinary Core Idea PS1.A: Structure and Properties of Matter.
- Science Process Standards 3 and 4: Planning and carrying out investigations; analyzing and interpreting data.
- Crosscutting Concepts: Energy and Matter.

It also addresses a Common Core reading standard:

• Draw on information from multiple print or digital sources, demonstrating the ability to locate an answer to a question quickly or to solve a problem efficiently. (CCSS.ELA-LITERACY.RI.5.7)

Here is the example.

> Our school wants to start a recycling program for plastic containers. The people in charge of the project wonder if they should collect plastics with all seven recycling codes or whether they should collect plastics with only a few of them. First, look up what the recycling code on the containers signifies about the chemical makeup of the plastic. Then, plan and carry out an experiment to test a hypothesis about the plastics' physical properties—specifically, how easy the plastics would be to crush and package for shipping. Use both what you looked up about the different plastics and the results of your experiment to recommend which plastics would be best to recycle.
>
> You will be assessed on your content knowledge about properties of matter, your ability to conduct experimental inquiry, your ability to make decisions and recommendations, and your ability to communicate effectively in a variety of ways.

First, let's analyze the task from the student's point of view to see if the performance assessment really taps the intended science inquiry skills: *The problem I have to solve is to find out the chemical and physical properties of each of the seven types of recyclable plastic. That means I have to know what "chemical properties" means. I also have to investigate to learn more about them, using the plastic-recycling codes. I have to design and conduct an experiment to figure out which plastics are physically the most recyclable. I've been given a topic for the experiment's hypothesis (ease of crushing and packaging) but no criteria as to how to value this compared with each plastic's chemical properties in regard to the decision about how recyclable each kind of plastic would be.*

The first task, looking up what the recycling codes mean, is at the Understand level of Bloom's taxonomy. It may sound like a task at the Analyze level, but a quick Internet search will locate information on the plastic-recycling codes and what they mean, including some information about the plastics' density and chemical composition. Students would have to compile and summarize information but would basically be reporting their understanding of facts already compiled for them in readily available resources. The students' higher-order thinking in this task occurs in designing and conducting the experiment and in reasoning from their results and the chemical information they looked up to make recommendations about recycling the plastics. Designing and conducting original experiments are at the Create level. Reasoning from the results to make recommendations, which involve identifying and prioritizing—that is, valuing—criteria, is at the Evaluate level. Our analysis of the task from the student's point of view demonstrates that what the students would have to do to perform the task does tap the intended learning outcomes.

Now let's consider how different aspects of this task have been controlled to make this happen. Chapter 6 talked about length and group work as two aspects of performance tasks that can vary. This task is of moderate length. It involves looking up information, designing and conducting an experiment, and synthesizing results from both activities into recommendations. Therefore, it would make visible students' abilities to engage in complex thinking, putting together several different thinking tasks into a whole and sensible project. No mention was made of group work, although it is worth noting that this task could be adapted to use multistep design, as described in the section on group work in Chapter 6. Formative assessment opportunities could be built into the phases of the project, and opportunities for individual summative assessment could be incorporated at the end.

We can use Figure 7.1 to analyze the task structure or amount of scaffolding presented in this task. The main problem is provided. The teacher has specified the main question (Which plastics are the best candidates for recycling?). The strategies and materials for answering this question are left more open. Students are guided in the strategies they will use, but there is room for their own reasoning and choice. Students are told to "look up" what the numeric codes mean, but they are not constrained as to how to do that. Most will probably use the Internet, but they could also use books and other print resources.

Similarly, students are instructed to design and carry out an experiment to test a physical property of the plastics, but they are free to design their own specific hypotheses, methods, and materials, and are left on their own to devise ways to gather, interpret, and report data. Here's the important point: if the choice of methods and materials had *not* been left somewhat open, this performance assessment would *not* have assessed the science inquiry standards as intended. If the teacher had provided lab manual–style directions for the experiment, students still could have been called on to use Evaluate-level thinking to reason from their results to prioritize plastics for recycling, but they would not have had to use Create-level thinking to do the experiments themselves.

Finally, this performance task does not provide students with directions for how to present the results of any of the three phases of the project: the information on plastics codes procured by looking them up, the experiment, or the recommendations. Students are free to decide how to present these results. This is true even if most students decide to present their final product in conventional ways—for example, in a report. Most students would probably decide to use conventional communication formats; after all, those formats' effectiveness is part of why they are conventional. The key is that students decide on which form to use, based on their purpose, and use it appropriately.

In summary, then, the amount of task structure in this task could be diagrammed as shown in Figure 7.2, following the categories in Figure 7.1.

Figure 7.2 Diagram of Task Structure: Science Example

Task Feature	Less Structure ◄——► More Structure		
Identify problem	Not Provided	Guided	**Provided**
Select and use strategies/materials	Not Provided	**Guided**	Provided
Present final product	**Not Provided**	Guided	Provided

Deliberately controlling the amount of task structure in the various aspects of the task ensured that the task matched its requirements related to content knowledge and higher-order thinking. Leaving the experimental design fairly open allowed for assessment of the science inquiry standards, whereas providing complete directions would not have done so. Leaving the final product open allowed for assessment of the science communication standards more broadly than would have been possible if the teacher had specified a particular format.

An Example in Mathematics

This math example aligns with Common Core standards in statistics and probability at the 6th grade level and several mathematical practices. The content knowledge students are expected to demonstrate is the ability to summarize numerical data sets in relation to their context by reporting the number of observations (CCSS.MATH.CONTENT.6.SP.B.5.A), giving quantitative measures of center (median and/or mean) (CCSS.MATH.CONTENT.6.SP.B.5.C), and relating the choice of measures of center and variability to the shape of the data distribution and the context in which the data were gathered (CCSS.MATH.CONTENT.6.SP.B.5.D). The practices being tapped include students' abilities to make sense of problems and persevere in solving them (CCSS.MATH.PRACTICE.MP1), to reason abstractly and quantitatively (CCSS.MATH.PRACTICE.MP2), and to construct viable arguments (CCSS.MATH.PRACTICE.MP3).

A problem set requiring students to calculate mean and median for several data sets could tap standards 6.SP.B.5.A and 6.SP.B.5.C, but to know how students relate choice of measures of central tendency to the shape of the distribution and to the context, we need a problem requiring thinking and explaining. Here is an example.

> Some friends play a word game on their cell phones. This week, they are having a contest and want to award first, second, and third prizes for Best Player. The friends have kept records of their scores. In the chart below, you will find the scores of three of the friends. Using what you know about measures of central tendency and any other mathematical reasoning you think is important here, make the case that any one of them could win the first prize for Best Player. Then tell who you think should win first prize and who should be second and third, explaining your reasoning. Show your calculations in the space for calculation work. Write your explanations in complete sentences, using mathematical vocabulary.

Name	Monday	Tuesday	Wednesday	Thursday	Friday
Armin	272	395	315	341	287
Joel	31	110	380	386	388
Sophia	315	315	315	315	316

Calculations:

Make the case that any one of these three students could win first prize as Best Player:

Who do you think should win first, second, and third prizes? Explain your reasoning:

As before, let's look at this from the student's point of view, which is the best way to tell what a task really assesses. *What is this task asking me to do? I am to figure out, using math, some way in which each of these friends is "best" at playing the word game. I can use any methods I want, but they have to include measures of central tendency. Then I should figure out how I think the students should be ranked for the prize. I have to explain my reasoning in written form for both of these undertakings.*

If all students needed to do was calculate each friend's mean and median scores for the week, the problem would require thinking at the Apply level. Students would be applying known algorithms to calculate these quantities, and there would be right and wrong answers. Using these results to evaluate the game-playing prowess of the three friends requires thinking at the Evaluate level. If students just had to explain the game skills of the three friends, the task would require thinking at the Analyze level. But students must use their analysis of the friends' game-playing results to rank them, which means placing more value on some criteria (e.g., highest mean) than others (e.g., highest median)—which in turn means thinking at the Evaluate level. Different students will approach this in different ways, and as long as their explanations make sense and use the appropriate mathematical concepts and vocabulary, their responses will be acceptable.

Again, let's look at features of the task and how they have been controlled. This is not a very long task. It could be completed in less than one class period. However, it is a complex task because it requires a combination of mathematical reasoning and problem solving, extended calculations, and written mathematical communication about two different but related matters. The task could have been made much less complicated by simplifying the reasoning. For example, the scenario and data table could have been used as introductory material for a series of questions such as "Which friend has the highest mean score?" and "Which friend has the highest median score?" Removing some of the complexity of the task in this fashion, however, would *change* the thinking skills assessed. Again, the important point to remember is that you can vary aspects of the task to control the level of thinking. The question of which task design is "best" is answered not by asking which design taps more higher-order thinking but by asking which taps the thinking called for in the learning standards you intend to assess.

This performance assessment makes no mention of group work. It is intended as an individual assessment. A good use of group work might be to have students work in groups during the learning of the skills this task assessed—for example, calculating medians and means and answering questions about how to interpret these values. Then, the performance assessment could be used to make individual students' thinking visible. One caution is in order. If you used a group instructional activity that was just like this one—for example, asking an analogous problem about ice cream sales—and then used this individual performance assessment afterward, the level of thinking required would be to *recall* the work that was done on the other problem and *apply* those strategies to this problem. The way to teach students to do mathematical reasoning is to ask them to do all sorts of different mathematical reasoning. When you make them repeat the same strategy, they are no longer analyzing; they are just applying what they already learned.

What about the amount of task structure in this performance assessment task? How was that controlled, and how did that control lead to the desired level of thinking? The problem itself is provided. The teacher has specified that the problem is to evaluate the game-playing skills of three friends. The strategies for doing that, however, are somewhat more open. The one piece of guidance students get is that they must use measures of central tendency as one of their strategies. They are free to use other relevant mathematical strategies; two that come to mind immediately are consistency of performance and increase in performance, but there are actually several "outside-the-box" strategies for approaching this problem that require using measures of central tendency as well. Students are left to themselves to decide on the strategies to use for evaluating each friend's evidence in terms of Best Player status. The directions for presenting the final answer are provided; students must put calculation work in one section and write paragraphs under two separate questions. In terms of the categories in Figure 7.1, the amount of task structure in this task could be diagrammed as shown in Figure 7.3.

Figure 7.3 Diagram of Task Structure: Mathematics Example

Task Feature	Less Structure ←		→ More Structure
Identify problem	Not Provided	Guided	**Provided**
Select and use strategies/materials	Not Provided	**Guided**	Provided
Present final product	Not Provided	Guided	**Provided**

Again, the important point to notice here is that the degree of openness of the task in terms of mathematical strategies and mathematical reasoning is what makes the task assess the higher-order thinking inherent in the mathematical practices. If the teacher had provided all of the directions, the task would not have stretched students' reasoning very far.

An Example in English Language Arts

For an English language arts example, let's consider a task that asks students to produce a piece of persuasive writing. This assessment taps at least two of the Common Core writing standards for grade 5:

- Write opinion pieces on topics or texts, supporting a point of view with reasons and information. (CCSS.ELA-LITERACY.W.5.1)
  - Introduce a topic or text clearly, state an opinion, and create an organizational structure in which ideas are logically grouped to support the writer's purpose. (W.5.1.A)
  - Provide logically ordered reasons that are supported by facts and details. (W.5.1.B)
  - Link opinion and reasons using words, phrases, and clauses (e.g., *consequently, specifically*). (W.5.1.C)
  - Provide a concluding statement or section related to the opinion presented. (W.5.1.D)
- Produce clear and coherent writing in which the development and organization are appropriate to task, purpose, and audience. (CCSS.ELA-LITERACY.W.5.4)

This performance assessment will take the form of a writing prompt with work over two days in class. On the first day, students will brainstorm ideas and then write a first draft. On the second day, students will self-assess their work using rubrics and then write a second draft to turn in to the teacher. Here is one way the teacher could structure the writing prompt.

School Uniforms

Teachers have noticed some students mocking or bullying other students, especially making fun of the clothes some students wear. The principal of our school is wondering whether she should ask the school board to institute a school uniform policy so that all students would be wearing the same clothes. Write an essay to the principal to persuade her that uniforms are, or are not, a good solution to this problem.

From the student point of view, the problem to solve is to decide whether to support or oppose a school uniform policy and to marshal a coherent written argument to that effect. This requires thinking at the Evaluate level. Students must analyze the school context as they know it and then evaluate whether uniforms would improve that context. The students would also need to follow the writing process, which is not part of the prompt but would be part of the task as carried out in the classroom. This is an individual task that would take no more than two class periods. It does not require the use of outside resources.

The task is very structured. The problem is given: students must take and support a position on school uniforms. The method is prescribed: students must develop their opinion and bring to bear supporting details using a certain writing process (brainstorming, first draft, self-assessment, second draft). The final product is prescribed: students must write an essay to the principal. The task's structure can be illustrated by the diagram in Figure 7.4.

Figure 7.4 Diagram of Task Structure: English Language Arts Example (Version 1)

Task Feature	Less Structure ◄	────	► More Structure
Identify problem	Not Provided	Guided	**Provided**
Select and use strategies/materials	Not Provided	Guided	**Provided**
Present final product	Not Provided	Guided	**Provided**

What if the teacher wanted to make the task more open? How might she do that? Which task features could be opened up and still result in students being assessed on the intended learning outcomes about writing clear and coherent opinion pieces? The best options for opening up the assessment to more student decision making would be to guide students in identifying the problem or in the strategies they will use to solve it instead of providing those aspects. One possibility might look like this.

School Reforms

The school board is interested in making the school a more comfortable place for students to study and learn. There have been all sorts of suggestions—for example, offering choices of activities during lunch, changing the locker policy, relaxing the dress code, and changing the bell schedule. The principal of our school does not know which of these suggestions, or maybe something else, would be most helpful in making the school more comfortable for students. Decide which change in school policy you think would most help students become more comfortable and thus able to study and learn better in school. Write an essay to the principal to persuade her that your suggestion is a good one and is the one she should take.

In this version of the task, the problem-identification feature has been opened up. Students are given a general problem (school reform) and must define their own specific problem—what exactly to write about. Given that the students are to be assessed in writing an opinion piece, the strategies and methods for writing (the writing process) and directions for the final product are not amenable to as much student choice. If the students must produce a written piece, according to the standard, then allowing them a choice of presenting their argument orally would not be appropriate. There is still a bit of wiggle room—for example, giving students the choice to write an essay or an editorial for the school newspaper. Such a choice, however, would not reap many benefits in terms of supporting students' higher-order thinking because the choice of an essay or editorial would not make a lot of difference in the final product. Loosening up the structure around designing the problem, however, does have an effect on the thinking students must do. This version of the task could require thinking at the Create level if, in addition to analyzing the context and evaluating various suggestions, students come up with their own suggestions. The diagram in Figure 7.5 illustrates the structure of our new task, which stretches students' minds a bit further than the original version.

The point of comparing two versions of the task is to illustrate that choices about task structure must serve two purposes: (1) they should provide for as much student thinking as is reasonable and relevant to the learning outcome you are trying to assess, and (2) they must help the task match the learning outcome, which often puts some constraints on how much openness you can design into a task.

Figure 7.5 Diagram of Task Structure: English Language Arts Example (Version 2)

Task Feature	Less Structure ◄		► More Structure
Identify problem	Not Provided	**Guided**	Provided
Select and use strategies/materials	Not Provided	Guided	**Provided**
Present final product	Not Provided	Guided	**Provided**

An Example in Social Studies

Let's use a social studies example to show how you can tailor what is assessed by changing a performance task and its structure, as we did for the English example. Two of the dimensions of the C3 Framework for Social Studies State Standards (NCSS, 2013) are (1) developing questions and planning inquiries and (2) applying disciplinary concepts and tools. The state of Kansas uses this framework (www.ksde.org). The 2013 Kansas Standards for History, Government, and Social Studies suggest a 7th grade unit in Kansas state history titled "Kansas: To the Stars Through Difficulty (1865–1890s)," in which students should, among other things, "investigate the romantic image of the West and compare and contrast that image with primary source evidence" (Kansas State Board of Education, 2013, p. 72). Figure 7.6 shows one piece of primary source evidence, from the Kansas Historical Society website (www.kansasmemory.org/item/219152). Additional photos are also available there, and a teacher could collect several primary-source photographs of one-room schoolhouses.

Now let's see how varying and controlling the amount of structure in a performance task using these documents changes the thinking students must use and, therefore, changes what is assessed. First let's consider a very structured performance task, with problem identification, strategies and materials, and directions for final product all provided.

Figure 7.6 Students in Front of Kansas Schoolhouse, c. 1870–1890

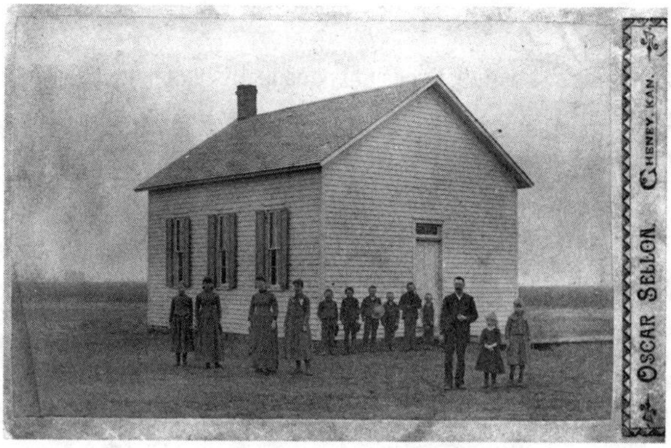

Source: Kansas State Historical Society, Item Number: 219152; Call Number: FK2.S3.76 *1; KSHS Identifier: DaRT ID: 219152. Reprinted with permission.

Look at the photo of the students and their one-room schoolhouse in Sedgwick County, Kansas. Take a similar photo of some students standing outside our school today. Working in groups of four, make a poster. On a piece of poster board, make a T-chart and mount these pictures at the top. Use the T-chart to compare and contrast elements of the photos that help us see how schooling today is similar to the way it was in the 1870s–1890s and how it is different. When your poster is complete, each person in the group should write his or her own essay about the experience of school then and now and what that might mean for the people of Kansas. You can use the books in our state history book display or the Internet to get more information about one-room schoolhouses.

From the point of view of the student, the problem to solve is to identify elements in each picture and reason from them to describe aspects of schooling. The main source of information is photographs, and additional information may be obtained from books or the Internet. Some group work (making the poster) is designed to get students thinking. The final product is an individual essay that will assess what students understand about one aspect of culture—education—in the designated time period. Comparison with students' own experiences of school today will allow students to use their larger understanding of schooling to help interpret the historical evidence. This task requires thinking at the Analyze level.

What if the teacher wanted to open up some of this task to more student decision making? She could, of course, just allow variations in format for its own sake—for example, allowing an essay or a photo album or a presentation for the final product. Although that might pique students' interest, it would not foster thinking *in the discipline* as much as opening up the problem, strategies and materials, or final product to student choices related to the content standards. Here is an example.

> Look at the photo of the students and their one-room schoolhouse in Sedgwick County, Kansas. Your job is to pretend you are one of those students and get as much information as you can about what it would have been like to go to that school or one like it. What sort of work would you do at school, and what would it be like to be in a class of students of all different ages? How do you think that school experience would have prepared you for your life in the community? Share your insights in a letter to a friend or a diary entry (remember, there was no texting or Facebook then!).

This task has loosened up the structure on all three task features. Problem definition, strategies and materials, and final product are all now *guided* instead of *provided*. The task is partly defined (what would it have been like to go to school then?), but the specifics are not constrained. Students are free to focus on various aspects of the one-room schoolhouse. The inquiry is guided, but exactly how students will approach the task of "finding as much as you can" is left to them. For example, some might choose to focus more on the academic work and some might focus more on the social aspects. Similarly, the strategies and materials are guided, but there is room for student decision making. The task does not specify where the students should locate information or how much information they should gather. Finally, the directions for the final product include some structure, but students have a choice between a letter or a diary entry, both historically appropriate forms of writing. This version of the task requires Evaluate-level thinking, because students must use the information they gather about the one-room schoolhouse to evaluate what sort of preparation for their life they think such an education would provide.

* * * * * *

Varying task structure is a powerful way to control what kind of thinking performance assessment tasks require of students. But, as you know, it is not the only way. In the next chapter, we take a look at two more aspects of performance assessment tasks that you can deliberately control and vary to match your assessment needs. In addition to intentionally varying task structure, you can control the *cognitive level* and the *difficulty* of a task by how you phrase the questions you ask.

8 Performance Assessment Tasks: Controlling Cognitive Level and Difficulty

As with all the other aspects of a task that I have discussed (length, group or individual work, amount of task structure), you should be able to intentionally control the cognitive level and the difficulty of a performance task so that it requires of students exactly the knowledge and skills you want to assess. In this book I have been using the cognitive-process dimension of the new Bloom's taxonomy (Anderson & Krathwohl, 2001), without much introduction, as a kind of shorthand for describing the cognitive level required by a particular performance assessment task. I have done this because I believe most readers are familiar enough with the categories in the taxonomy to find them useful. Although I describe the new Bloom's taxonomy more fully in this chapter, the main purpose of this discussion is to describe how you can vary performance assessment tasks to control the level of thinking a performance task requires. I also describe strategies for varying the difficulty level of a performance task and make the point that cognitive level and difficulty are two different things.

Cognitive Level

It's important to realize that Bloom's is not the only thinking-skills taxonomy you can use. Several others are commonly used, such as Webb's Depth of Knowledge levels (Webb, 2002) and the SOLO (Structure of Observed Learning Outcome) taxonomy (Biggs & Collis, 1982). Webb's taxonomy is often used in studies of the alignment of large-scale tests with the standards they are intended to assess. The SOLO taxonomy classifies the cognitive complexity of a learning task and a student's response and the kind of relationships a learner can make between elements of a task. I use Bloom—or, more precisely, the revised Bloom's taxonomy (Anderson & Krathwohl, 2001)—here because of its familiarity.

The revised Bloom's taxonomy is a classification system for educational outcomes using two dimensions: Knowledge and Cognitive Process. The Knowledge dimension acknowledges four types of knowledge: factual, conceptual, procedural, and metacognitive. This dimension was added for the revision; the original Bloom's taxonomy (Bloom et al., 1956) consisted only of levels of thinking (Cognitive Process). Those who revised the taxonomy realized that there were different kinds of knowledge. Knowing that $2 \times 2 = 4$ (factual knowledge), for example, is different from knowing an algorithm for doing division (procedural knowledge). Both are different from understanding the relationship between multiplication and division (conceptual knowledge) or from understanding when you have trouble distinguishing problems calling for multiplication from those calling for division (metacognitive knowledge).

In this book, I have been using the Cognitive Process dimension because it is useful for distinguishing the kind of mental work students must do to accomplish various tasks. This dimension starts with "remembering" some piece of knowledge. Cognition increases in complexity as students have to do more and more with that piece of knowledge. Before we review the definitions of the new Bloom Cognitive Process categories, it is worth cautioning that this dimension, although hierarchical, does *not* mean that "higher-order" thinking is more difficult than recall; nor does it mean that higher-order thinking is "better" than recall. Finally, asking a question or setting a task that requires higher-order thinking does not guarantee that a student will use that kind of thinking. You still need to review the student's response and assess the quality of thinking. This is why rubrics need to take into account the kind of thinking students do if assessing higher-order thinking was part of your intent (Brookhart, 2013b).

Notwithstanding all these caveats, which I feel compelled to make because Bloom's or any other taxonomy can be misused and cause harm to student learning, the Cognitive Process dimension of the revised Bloom's taxonomy is a useful tool when designing a performance assessment task. Unless a question or task calls for a certain level of thinking, students will not have an opportunity to exhibit that level of thinking. Here are the categories and their definitions (Anderson & Krathwohl, 2001):

- Remember—Retrieve knowledge from memory.
- Understand—Construct meaning from oral, written, and graphic communications.
- Apply—Use a procedure in a situation for which it is appropriate.
- Analyze—Break down material into elements, decide how the elements relate to one another and to an overall structure or purpose.
- Evaluate—Make judgments based on criteria.
- Create—Put elements together to form a new whole.

This dimension is hierarchical in the sense that cognitive processing at any given level also involves activity at the levels below it. For example, to *analyze* a short story in order to determine the structure of the plot, a reader also needs to *remember* some facts about plot, *understand* the story, and *apply* the conventional dramatic structure to the elements of the short story the reader has pulled out for analysis. The convention is to designate a question or task at the highest level of cognitive processing it requires, realizing that other levels will be involved as well.

Why is understanding and categorizing cognitive process important for designing performance assessment tasks? Because if you know what level of cognitive processing you intend for students to learn to do, you can write tasks that call upon that level of processing—provided you know what to ask for. The taxonomy helps you know what to ask for.

For example, the Common Core includes the following grade 9–10 standard for reading informational text:

> Analyze seminal U.S. documents of historical and literary significance (e.g., Washington's Farewell Address, the Gettysburg Address, Roosevelt's Four Freedoms speech, King's "Letter from Birmingham Jail"), including how they address related themes and concepts. (CCSS.ELA-LITERACY.RI.9-10.9)

Clearly, the standard says "Analyze." And clearly, the elements readers should be able to pull from the texts include "related themes and concepts." What would a task that called for such analysis look like? Appendix B to the Common Core State Standards for English Language Arts includes the following sample performance task aligned with the standard:

> Students compare George Washington's Farewell Address to other foreign policy statements, such as the Monroe Doctrine, and *analyze* how both texts *address similar themes and concepts* regarding "entangling alliances."

What does this sample task provide that the standard itself does not? Let's draw on our discussion of task structure from Chapter 7. First, this sample performance assessment sets up a problem—namely, to compare George Washington's Farewell Address to other documents. In terms of the framework we have been using, the problem is guided, not completely provided. Students are free to choose the foreign policy documents for comparison to Washington's address. The task includes one suggestion, and it does not specify the number of documents students might choose for the comparison.

The task also provides guidance for the strategies students will use in their analysis. Specifically, they need to pull out elements from each foreign policy document they use that consider "entangling alliances." The task provides no directions for the final product. However, because this sample performance task appeared in a list of examples in an appendix to the Common Core English language arts standards, it was not necessarily meant as a complete set of directions for a performance task. Teachers who were using this performance task would need to add more directions, including criteria for assessment, and could add more structure in any of the aspects of the task if they wished.

The sample performance task shows a match with the cognitive level required by the standard (Analyze) and the cognitive level required by the performance task.

Using the taxonomy helps us see the match. Using the taxonomy also helps us see the mismatch inherent in tasks such as the following.

> Read Washington's Farewell Address. What is his advice on alliances with foreign nations? What reasons did he give for this position?

This question requires thinking at the Understand level. The information necessary to answer the question is contained in the address, which is actually an open letter to the American people published in newspapers in 1796. Questions like this one might be part of the larger instructional sequence related to the standard, but they will not provide assessment evidence of achievement of the standard. Such evidence requires a match with both content and thinking skills.

Let's try another example, this time with a standard that does *not* so clearly specify one intended level of cognitive complexity. Many standards are written about content with the implied (or sometimes stated) intention that students should be able to approach that content at many different levels of thinking. Some standards are written about content but have cross-cutting "practice" standards (e.g., the Common Core State Standards for Mathematics or the Next Generation Science Standards). These practices require higher-order thinking at different levels (Analyze, Evaluate, Create) and are intended to be addressed whenever possible with different content standards.

I'll select a Common Core standard for 4th grade Numbers and Operations in Base Ten because I think readers will be familiar with the content, making it easier to illustrate task adjustments that change the cognitive level. Here is the standard:

> Fluently add and subtract multi-digit whole numbers using the standard algorithm. (CCSS.MATH.CONTENT.4.NBT.B.4)

If this content standard were read by itself, it would require thinking at the Apply level. Students would need to know the standard algorithms for adding and subtracting multi-digit whole numbers (procedural knowledge) and be able to apply those strategies to any given problem, such as these:

$$\begin{array}{r} 324 \\ +\ 298 \\ \hline \end{array} \qquad \begin{array}{r} 856 \\ -\ 483 \\ \hline \end{array}$$

If students could do exercises that looked like this, at a reasonable level of accomplishment (say, 80 percent), we might be tempted to say they had met the standard. However, the content standards are meant to be read alongside the practice standards. The first Common Core mathematical practice standard reads, "Make sense of problems and persevere in solving them" (CCSS.MATH.PRACTICE.MP1). The first part, making sense of problems, can be assessed at several different cognitive levels. The second part, persevering in solving problems, is not so much a cognitive activity as it is a motivational one; however, as students realize (cognitively) that they have the knowledge and skills they need to solve problems, they will be more likely to persevere in solving them (Pajares, 2006).

One way to assess what sense students make of problems is to ask them to show their work and explain their reasoning. This is a step beyond the "show your work" directions my math teachers gave me when I was in school. Showing work, even work that is correct, neat, and easy to follow, does not guarantee that the student understands the reasoning behind the process. The student could be simply following a procedure that was taught in class. Consider a performance assessment such as the following.

> Farmer Jones collected eggs from the henhouse every morning. On Monday, he collected 312 eggs. On Tuesday, he collected 15 more eggs than he did on Monday. On Wednesday, he collected 27 fewer eggs than he did on Tuesday. How many eggs did he collect in the three days? Show your work and explain your reasoning.

Just solving this problem, itself, represents reasoning at the Apply level. Although the problem has several steps (Tuesday eggs = 312 + 15, or 327; Wednesday eggs = 327 − 27, or 300; 312 + 327 + 300 = 939), each step is an application of a standard algorithm for addition or subtraction. Showing the work would confirm that the student identified which numbers to add or subtract and performed the calculations properly. Explaining reasoning, however, would require the student to communicate how she conceptualized the problem (e.g., "I needed to add 15 more eggs to 312"), describe what elements of the problem she paid attention to at each step, and give reasons. This requires thinking at the Analyze level. Criteria for assessing the response should include more than correct application of the standard algorithm and correct calculation. The response should also be assessed with a criterion for mathematical reasoning, or a criterion for mathematical communication that included "telling what I did and why I did it."

Consider another problem that uses multi-digit subtraction, requires students to make sense of a problem, also requires students to reason abstractly and quantitatively (CCSS.MATH.PRACTICE.MP2), and is written at the Evaluate level.

David and Huan are playing a subtraction game. Their goal is to create a subtraction problem that will have the largest answer. They have game pieces numbered 1 through 5, and each student has placed two of the pieces and has three (2, 3, and 4) left:

DAVID	HUAN
1 __ __	__ __ 5
− 5 __	− __ 1
______	______

Which boy has used a more effective strategy for winning the game? Explain why.

Again, this problem requires knowledge of the standard algorithm for multi-digit subtraction. But it also requires making sense of the problem (in this case, identifying place value as an important element as well), and using that understanding to reason quantitatively (David, who put the 1 in the hundreds place, has constrained his answer to be less than 100, whereas Huan will have an answer that is greater than 100). Finally, this problem requires recognizing the criterion by which "a more effective strategy" should be judged—namely, arriving at the largest difference—and explaining why that means Huan's strategy is more effective than David's.

It is also possible to assess students on the content standard of fluently adding and subtracting multi-digit whole numbers using the standard algorithm as well as on the mathematical practices of making sense of a problem and reasoning quantitatively, requiring thinking at the Create level. I'm sure you can think of several examples. Here is one.

> Write a word problem that requires addition or subtraction of numbers greater than 10 in order to solve it. Then solve the problem, show your work, and explain your reasoning.

In terms of task structure, this problem provides very little scaffolding. Teachers could list suggested problem contexts (e.g., school, shopping, sports) if they wanted to provide more structure. Criteria for assessing student responses should include, in addition to mathematical concepts and calculations, whether the student had created a problem appropriate for use with addition or subtraction and the quality of the mathematical explanation.

The purpose of providing three examples of performance tasks, all for the same standard but at different cognitive levels, is to illustrate how your choices on task design affect exactly what is assessed with any given performance task. Each of the three examples assesses student understanding of addition and subtraction, but different levels of thinking. The choices you make about what level of thinking your tasks require should be intentional, aligned with standards (in this case, both content and mathematical practices) and with the level of thinking you want students to exhibit. Then, the criteria for what to look for in student responses should reflect these requirements, so you have a way to assess whether students did, in fact, exhibit the kind of thinking you asked for.

Difficulty

This section has two messages. One is that difficulty is not the same as cognitive level. Prepare tasks for students that are at an appropriate level of difficulty for them but that require a range of levels of thinking. The second message is about how to vary and control the difficulty level in the performance tasks you design.

Difficulty and Cognitive Level: Two Different Things

Difficulty and cognitive level are related—in general, the more complex a task, the more difficult it might be—but they are by no means the same. Tasks at the Remember level can be very difficult, and many tasks at the Analyze, Evaluate, or Create level can be very easy. The first point in this section, then, is simply to convince you that difficulty is not the same as cognitive level. I hope these examples will do it.

Remember-level questions:

- What does the word *thankful* mean? (easy)
- What does the word *incunabulum* mean? (difficult)

Higher-order thinking tasks:

- Write your own fable with the moral "Gratitude is the sign of noble souls." (easy)
- Write an epic poem in the style of Homer that is a prequel to the *Iliad.* (difficult)

In these examples, both higher-order thinking tasks require Create-level thinking, but no matter what the level of thinking, it is simply not true that "higher-order" means "more difficult." The reason this is important to me is an equity issue. Well-meaning teachers who truly believe that students have to master facts before they can move on to thinking routinely shortchange students. Lower-achieving students can and do benefit from higher-order thinking (Pogrow, 2005). Sometimes teachers, in the name of differentiation, will tell me that they will reserve exercises that require higher-order thinking for their advanced students. This makes me sad! All students should be presented with tasks that require higher-order thinking. Students who are remanded to doing only endless drill-and-practice exercises get bored, don't see the point of school, and drop out—and I can't really blame them.

Two Factors That Influence the Difficulty of a Task

Students' *experience* of the difficulty of a task rests on two factors: the students themselves and the contents and nature of the task. For example, if you gave me a really simple Greek-to-English translation exercise, I would find it enormously difficult because I don't read Greek. If you gave the same simple exercise to someone who did read Greek, that person might find it much easier than reading a complex text in the same language. To control the difficulty level of a performance assessment task, you need to attend to both student readiness and the nature of the task itself.

Student factors. Students find their "way in" to a task based on prior knowledge, prior experiences and relationships, and their interests and expectancies. For example, when I was in the 8th grade, our social studies class studied American history. When we arrived at the Civil War unit, we realized that one of our classmates was a Civil War hobbyist. He had read piles of books on the subject; built models of battles, camps, and weaponry; and participated in re-enactments. Our Civil War unit, which was probably of average difficulty to most of us in the class, was a piece of cake for him.

More generally, students who have participated in sound instruction and formative assessment, who have been given enough background information to handle a task, and who are comfortable working in the topic area will experience the same task as much less difficult than students who have not been well prepared for it. To adjust the difficulty of a task, create tasks that differ in their requirements for prior knowledge, experiences, and interests. To stretch students to do work that is more difficult, design a task that is a step beyond where they are currently working, not a giant leap.

Task factors. Holding student background and experience constant, some factors about the task itself can influence difficulty level. To understand these, you need to be an expert in teaching in a discipline and understand the learning progressions in that discipline. For example, students who can count to 20 by 1s may find the idea of counting by 5s difficult. As this example illustrates, though, difficulty is still relative to a student's readiness. More advanced students would not find counting by 5s difficult at all. Nevertheless, the acquisition of subject-matter learning often involves something of an order, and that, in turn, influences the difficulty of a task.

Reading level or, more generally, level of difficulty of materials is an important aspect of task design that influences difficulty. However, difficulty of materials is relatively easy to adjust. To differentiate a research task into more and less difficult versions, sometimes all that is required is to offer more and less difficult resources for students to consult.

Beyond these two general factors, research about specific tasks in specific disciplines has unpacked the nature of difficulty for those specific tasks. For example, Bloomfield and her colleagues (2010) investigated factors that make comprehension in second-language listening more and less difficult. Koedinger (2010) illustrated a process of using think-alouds to identify difficulty factors in different tasks or classes of tasks, especially for mathematics. In fact, a whole field in the learning sciences is devoted to examining what makes problems difficult, how students process various task characteristics and hints, and how much instruction is optimal for resolving student difficulties. The important points for our purposes here are that factors that make a task "difficult" will in part be characteristics of the task or problem itself, that what these factors are will differ for different topics, and that one of the best ways to find out what students are thinking and how difficult they find the task is to ask them.

Mathematics Example

Here's an example of varying the difficulty level in a very obvious way in a mathematics problem that requires thinking at the Create level. The mathematical idea assessed is that the same algebraic expression can be related to different real-world situations, and it reflects Common Core math content standards 3.OA and 4.OA and practice standards MP1, MP2, and MP4 (Small, 2012, p. 161).

Easier example:
Write two different situations that could be described by the equation $4 \times [\ ] = 48$.

More difficult example:
Write two different situations that could be described by the equation $29 \times [\ ] = 377$.

The easier example requires multiplying by only one digit, which makes it easier from a content perspective. It also may be easier from a context perspective because students may be able to envision common scenarios with 48 "things" (crayons, cookies, students, cars) more easily than common scenarios involving 377 things.

Social Studies Example

In a geography class, one of the objectives is that students will be able to explain how physical characteristics of a place influenced human activities, such as agriculture, transportation, art and architecture, and economic activity in the ancient world (from Maryland Geography Standard 3.0, grade 6). Students are to prepare a report discussing the influence of geography on their chosen ancient civilization.

Select an ancient civilization in one of the following locations:

- Mesopotamia
- Africa, including Egypt
- Nubia/Kush and Sub-Saharan Africa
- Indus River Valley
- Northern China
- Greece or Rome
- Mesoamerica, such as the Incas, Mayans, and Aztecs

Prepare a report to answer the question "How did the geography of the place where they lived influence the work, life, and art of this civilization?"

[Additional directions about location of resources, time line, and format of final report or presentation would follow.]

This performance task should require thinking at the Analyze level. Students should need to locate resources about their chosen civilization, read those resources to pick out the relevant elements—information that relates geography to life in that civilization—and then organize these elements under the main points they will make in their report. Resist the temptation to make a less difficult version of this task by supplying an easy-reading resource that presents such information for one civilization and having lower-achieving students simply summarize it. This would require thinking only at the Understand level.

This task has several aspects that you can vary, however, to keep it at the Analyze level but make it less difficult for lower-achieving students or more challenging for more advanced students. The first aspect is the choice of reading material. Review the resources available in your classroom or school library for each civilization and identify the reading levels. Help students select a civilization where the resources they find will be at an appropriate level of challenge for their reading ability.

For students for whom a deep dive into an array of resources might be overwhelming, you might consider preselecting a set of resources in a few areas, perhaps for civilizations where a multitude of resources with pictures as well as text are available in a variety of formats—Egypt, Greece, or Rome, for example. For students who have difficulty focusing when the array of choices gets too large, you can offer a more constrained set of choices with preselected resources.

Another aspect of the task where you can vary the difficulty level is in the nature of the final product. For students who might find writing a report difficult, offer other formats—for example, preparing a PowerPoint presentation or a captioned picture book.

The important principle to note here is that the core task remains the same for each student. All have to locate information about the effects of geography on the development of ancient civilizations. All have to review resources for those elements of information and distinguish between geography-related information and other information. All have to organize what they learned into some sort of report. The standard indicates that students have to learn that geography influenced life in ancient civilizations. The standard does *not* indicate how difficult we should make it for students to do that.

One final word, in case you're wondering. If difficult "doesn't matter," then why not let everyone do the "easy" version of a task? Ah, but difficulty does matter. The students who are reading the more challenging texts, the students who are wading into and making sense of more disparate collections of resources, the students who are writing more detailed reports are learning important skills. Plus, they are enjoying the motivational benefits that come with approaching a challenging task and meeting that challenge. The level of challenge for students doing the less difficult version of the task is about the same *for them* as the level is for students doing the more difficult version. The key is to offer an appropriate level of challenge to as many students as possible while still holding fast to the content knowledge and skills to be attained and assessed. The result should be that all students learn as much as possible, show themselves in their best light on the assessment, and are ready for the "next notch up" in research and report writing—wherever that is for them—in their next assignment.

9 An Idea Bank of Performance Assessment Tasks

In this chapter, I have created an idea bank of sorts by assembling some suggestions for how to write performance tasks that tap higher-order thinking in various disciplines. Each bullet item is a separate suggestion, and I have grouped them into categories.

I provide this idea bank with great trepidation, because resources like this can easily be used as "cookbooks." It won't do to simply grab a template from the list below and plug in your topic of the day. Good design of performance tasks requires all the steps outlined in preceding chapters, and it starts with defining what you want to assess. Good design does *not* start with identifying an interesting activity from a list like the ones in this chapter.

However, I have decided to include this idea bank because many teachers find such suggestions helpful. For some, the step between knowing what they want to assess and actually writing the task is a large one. So let's make a deal. I'll present the idea bank to help people who need ideas about how to write, and you, the reader, will promise to use it thoughtfully and always start from your intended learning outcome, *not* any suggestion in these lists, when you are designing a performance assessment task. Use the idea bank to help you brainstorm tasks that match the content knowledge and skills and the higher-order thinking skills you want to assess. Also note that the ideas in this bank are at the early-development stage. To make them performance assessment tasks, you would need to flesh them out with complete directions for students. Some would need you to provide materials, planning sheets, library or Internet access, and other supplemental resources.

Also, please remember that this is an idea bank for creating the performance tasks only. Each task would need a rubric or other scoring scheme that matched the intended learning outcome directly and that could be used for giving formative feedback and also for giving a summative grade. To illustrate this point, I have included a sample rubric with the first idea in the bank, but remember that all of these tasks need rubrics to be complete performance assessments.

Working with Informational Text in Language Arts, Social Studies, Science, and Technical Subjects

When using these suggestions for informational text, be sure to distinguish between literal comprehension and higher-order thinking. Reporting on an idea explicitly stated in a text requires literal comprehension (Understand-level thinking). If students need to figure out something from the text, they are making an inference. You can't always tell from the question. For example, in some texts, "identify the main idea" requires literal comprehension, because the text says something like "The purpose of this article is to show you how tigers are becoming endangered." In other texts, finding the main idea depends on making inferences because the main idea is not stated directly.

Here are some suggestions for assessment tasks for informational text, with a rubric included for the first one:

- What is the main idea of [this text]? Support your answer by giving details or information from [this text]. Explain how these details support the main idea.

Possible criterion and rubrics for assessment: Does the student identify the main point and clearly support it with evidence from the text?

2 = Completely and Clearly—Main idea is clearly stated, and evidence from the passage is accurate, relevant, and complete. Explanation is clear.

1 = Partially—Main idea is stated but not well supported with evidence from the passage. Explanation is not completely clear.

0 = No—Main idea is not stated, or is not correct. Evidence from the passage is missing. Explanation is not clear.

- How is [this text] organized? Why do you think the author used that method of organizing [this text]? Explain your thinking.
- Give students several visual organizers (e.g., steps in a procedure, a concept web, and a compare/contrast Venn diagram) and ask, Which one of these is the best way to diagram [this text]? Explain why you chose that diagram.
- Which facts or concepts in [this text] are the most compelling evidence for the author's point? Explain your thinking.
- Which facts or concepts in [this text] surprised you, and why?
- Did the author of [this text] leave out some facts or concepts you wanted to know? What were they, and why do you think they were not in [this text]?
- What do you think the author of [this text] was trying to accomplish?
- Why do you think this author wrote [this text]? What kind of readers did the author write for, and what does the author want them to think after reading [this text]?
- How well do you think [this text] accomplishes what the author set out to do?
- What point of view does the author have about [text's topic or issue]? How do you know?
- How does the author support the argument [or message] [that…]? Does the author's reasoning make sense?
- What other point(s) do you think the author could have made to make a stronger case for [author's message]?
- What assumptions does the author make? OR What has to be true for the author's logic to be reasonable?
- Are there any irrelevant details? OR Is there any information in [this text] that does not seem to support [author's message]?
- Ask about word choice, connotations, descriptions, explanations, imagery, use of loaded words, and so on, depending on the text. Ask the questions as simply as possible. *Example:* Why do you think the author began the article by saying, "It's a sickness that slams you like a hammer"? What reactions did the author hope to get from the readers?

- Ask what questions *students* have after reading an article or part of an article. *Example* (after reading an article about Mayan houses): Suppose you had a chance to visit someone in a house like the one described in the article. What questions would you have before you go? What questions would you ask the person you visit? Explain why you want to know the answers to these questions.
- Ask students to identify questions they have for more information or insight into the topic or issue in the text. Then have them use these questions for library and Internet research.

You can assess even more higher-order thinking when you ask students to connect two or more texts. Think of "text" broadly: another reading passage that you supply—especially if the passages approach the same issue differently; the student's own life and experiences; situations or scenarios known to the students (e.g., connecting informational text about a U.S. presidential election with a current student council election in the school). Here are some examples:

- Both of [these texts] are about [topic]. How is the issue [or problem, or principle] of [topic] in the first text like the issue [or problem, or principle] of [topic] in the second text? How is it different? Support your ideas with details from the text.
- Both of [these texts] are about [topic]. Compare the two authors' points of view about [topic]. How are they alike, and how are they different? Which author's point of view do you find most persuasive [or compelling, or logical, or valuable] and why?
- Both of [these texts] are about [topic], but the authors make their cases differently. [Then ask about similarities and differences in the organization of the texts, or of the kinds of evidence presented. Or ask which one is more persuasive or believable and why.]

Problem Solving in Mathematics or Science

Almost any conventional mathematics problem or math-based science problem (e.g., a problem about volume or temperature) can be turned into a performance assessment if you ask students to show their work *and explain their reasoning.* Many students are used to "showing their work"; in fact, in doing many math problems by hand it is necessary to include the work. However, explaining reasoning goes one step beyond showing work and raises the cognitive level of the problem. Most math problems are at the Apply level of Bloom's taxonomy, as students apply known procedures to solve particular kinds of problems. Asking students to articulate what kind of problem they are solving and why they took each step in the solution requires them to *analyze* the problem and their own thinking. It also requires mathematical communication.

Understanding of Scientific Inquiry

Science practices are the core of "doing" science. Even young children can be asked to find patterns and classify things. For example, you could ask children to bring in as many different leaves as they can find; then, in groups, have them decide on one or more different ways they could classify the leaves. As students mature as scientists, they can learn and be assessed on their facility with classic science inquiry practices. Here are some examples:

- Ask students to classify hypotheses as testable or untestable, and to explain their reasoning.
- For a specific hypothesis, ask students to identify what is already known about the question and how they found that out.
- Ask students to design an experiment and defend their selection of independent, dependent, and control variables.
- Ask students to use what they know about a natural phenomenon to predict what might happen under certain conditions.
- Ask students to design an observation method to get data needed for a test of a particular hypothesis, and to explain their reasoning.
- Ask students to select the most appropriate representation of data for a given purpose, and to explain their reasoning.
- Ask students to write scientific explanations including a claim, evidence, and reasoning.

Understanding of Historical Methods

Students should learn that history isn't a "given" but is a construction of historians who apply historical methods to various artifacts and sources for any given event. There are often several different interpretations of historical events and the actions of historical figures, depending on what evidence is examined and how it is interpreted. As with the scientific method, students can learn historical methods by participating in them, and you can assess the quality of their work with performance assessments. Here are some examples:

- Give students, or have students write, a question of historical interest; then have them identify sources of relevant information, distinguishing between primary and secondary sources.
- Give students, or have students locate, a series of sources on a question of historical interest; then have them critique the sources as to credibility and potential bias, explaining their reasoning.
- Give, or have students write, a question of historical interest, locate and evaluate possible sources of information, and then select and organize the information into a historical narrative that is as objective and well documented as possible.

Understanding of Concepts in the Disciplines

Performance tasks are a natural fit for assessing students' discipline-related *skills*. For example, to assess whether a student can prepare a slide to be viewed under a microscope, ask the student to do just that. But well-crafted performance assessments can also assess students' discipline-related *understanding*:

- Ask students to construct something or to demonstrate an application of a principle (e.g., build an electric circuit that works).
- Ask students to construct a model or representation of a concept, a principle, a phenomenon, or an event. Examples include mapping a narrative; diagramming scientific or historical processes; making scale models of systems; representing the same concept in multiple ways (equation, data table, graph, words); or creating an appropriate metaphor or analogy for a process, an event, or a principle.

Gathering and Interpreting Information in Language Arts, Social Studies, Science, and Technical Subjects

Conventional reports and many other assignments can be wonderful opportunities for students to pose a meaningful question in a discipline and gather and interpret information to answer their question. Or such assignments can be empty exercises, requiring that the student simply look up information and cut-and-paste it into presentation slides or paragraphs. Make sure your information-gathering assignments require students to exercise higher-order thinking. Here are some examples:

- Give students a research question (e.g., "What was the life of an actor like in Shakespeare's time?" or "Do stars have life cycles?") and ask them to gather and synthesize information to answer it, organizing the information so that it makes sense to a reader.
- Alternatively, give students a topic (e.g., Shakespeare or stars) and ask them to find out enough about the topic to formulate their own research question within the topic area. Then ask them to gather and synthesize information to answer their question, organizing the information so that it makes sense to a reader. Scaffold as much as you need to (see Chapter 7); for example, you might tell students they have to organize their comparison and contrast information in a chart, or you might ask them to decide what the best way is to organize or display the information they find.

A WebQuest is a special case of an assignment that involves gathering and organizing information. Dodge and his colleagues (webquest.org) define a WebQuest as an inquiry lesson in which most of the information comes from the Internet. A true WebQuest task makes use of the Internet as more than just a repository of information, requires higher-order thinking, and is based on a scaled-down version of a task that adults do as citizens or workers (Dodge, 2002).

The *WebQuest Taskonomy: A Taxonomy of Tasks* (Dodge, 2002) works for WebQuests, but the categories are also useful for providing suggestions for student inquiry using all kinds of resources: the Internet, books and periodicals, and personal interviews. In the list that follows, I annotate the categories from the WebQuest Taskonomy with examples that could be used to help students gather and interpret information from multiple sources. Again, of course, any errors or omissions are mine. It is important to remember that students' gathering of information is key to all of these tasks, even those in which students are asked to take a position or create something novel.

- *Retelling Tasks:* Dodge (2002) acknowledges that you *can* ask students to gather information and report on it, but that most often these types of tasks don't tap higher-order thinking. They can be a good introduction to how to use the Internet or how to develop background information. *I don't recommend retelling tasks as a good use of performance assessment time;* I include the category here just for the sake of completeness of the list. If you start to design a retelling task, see if you can push it to become a compilation task.

- *Compilation Tasks:* Students gather information from multiple sources and filter and format that information to serve a specific purpose. You can give the students the purpose and format or let them design their own.
  - Compile a first-aid manual for students who are going mountain biking in North Carolina.
  - Develop plans for planting and maintaining a vegetable garden that will grow well and yield tasty food in [chosen location].
  - Curate a virtual museum exhibition to showcase [an artist's work, a period in art or music history, a period in American history, an ecosystem, a class of life (e.g., marine mammals)].

- *Mystery Tasks:* Students solve a puzzle that cannot be solved by just looking up a fact, but rather requires synthesizing information from several sources.
  - Who was Robin Hood?
  - Why did dinosaurs become extinct?
  - Was there really a lost city of Atlantis?

- *Journalistic Tasks:* Students cover an event in history or in the history of science or the arts by reporting it as a journalist would (for a newspaper, magazine, television or radio, a news website, etc.). To help make these kinds of tasks successful, work with students to understand things such as credibility of sources, bias, and point of view.
  - The 2008 presidential election

- The trial and death of Socrates
- Hurricane Katrina

• *Design Tasks:* Students design a product or a plan of action that solves a problem (someone actually needs the product or plan, and the design deals with known restrictions of time, budget, and so on).

- Develop a recycling plan for your school.
- Build a model glider that will go at least 30 feet.

• *Creative Product Tasks:* Students create a poem, skit, song, game—any creative format can be used—that illustrates their understanding of a particular topic.

- Paint a painting in the Cubist style.
- Write a skit illustrating what happened "behind closed doors" during the Yalta Conference.
- Write a poem expressing how Jesse feels at the end of *Bridge to Terabithia*.

• *Consensus-Building Tasks:* Students examine a controversy, attempt to understand and summarize conflicting points of view, and then draw a well-reasoned conclusion.

- Interview teachers, parents, and students and present a "policy white-paper" to give to your principal on the topic "Should cell phones be allowed in school?"

• *Persuasion Tasks:* Students investigate an issue, take a position, identify an audience that does not share that position, and write or present an argument to persuade the audience to adopt their opinion.

- Write a letter persuading the school board to [limit school football teams to high schools, increase the budget for field trips, etc.].
- Make a video advertisement persuading fast-food consumers that trans fats are not healthful and should be avoided.

• *Self-Knowledge Tasks:* Students gather information and reflect on its relevance to their own lives, thoughts and feelings, or goals and future.

- Gather information about one of the branches of the armed services, and report on how what you have found out fits or does not fit with your own strengths and goals, writing the results as a report titled "Is the Army [or Navy, Marines, etc.] for Me?"

– Keep a reader-response journal as you read a novel, and when you have finished the book, summarize how it connected with you on a personal level, using details from your journal to support your conclusions.

- *Analytical Tasks:* Students compare and contrast aspects or elements of two different things, and draw a meaningful conclusion.
  – How are the protagonists in [two pieces of literature] alike and different?
  – What are the similarities and differences between the threat of extinction faced by the Philippine eagle and the former threat faced by the bald eagle? Are some of the lessons learned from removing the bald eagle from the endangered species list helpful in thinking about strategies to help the Philippine eagle? Final products could be in various formats (reports, presentations, etc.).

- *Judgment Tasks:* Students choose from a limited list of positions, supporting their judgment both by reasoning and evidence and by articulating the values or criteria they applied to arrive at their positions.
  – Was the Marshall Plan a success?
  – Should the United States send astronauts to land on the moon again?

- *Scientific Tasks:* Students create hypotheses based on scientific information, design experiments to test the hypotheses, gather and analyze data, and interpret results and draw conclusions.
  – What is the effect of different watering schedules on the growth of [some species of plant]?
  – What are the effects of salinity and temperature on the surface tension of water?

* * * * * *

I hope this idea bank helps you come up with even more ideas for designing performance assessment tasks than I have listed here. Think of this chapter as part of a brainstorming exercise. And remember, the important thing is not picking a task from a list, but identifying a task that assesses exactly the content and thinking skills you need to assess. Using this idea bank should be more of a matching exercise for you than a "pick-your-favorite" exercise.

10 | Managing Assessment of Higher-Order Thinking

This book has addressed one aspect of assessing higher-order thinking—namely, how to design and write questions and tasks that require higher-order thinking in student responses. Writing questions and tasks is important enough, I believe, to merit a whole book, but there is more to instruction and assessment than just the questions. This chapter contains some final thoughts about the book you have just read and about some of the context you will need to put around assessment of higher-order thinking if it is to become a routine in your daily teaching. I'll start by summarizing the principles for writing questions and tasks that assess higher-order thinking (the focus of this book), and then I'll zoom out to talk about managing instructional planning with these higher-order thinking tasks in mind, and managing resources and student behavior when students are performing higher-order thinking tasks.

Principles for Assessing Higher-Order Thinking: A Summary

I began this book by arguing for the importance of assessing higher-order thinking and by providing the heuristic of looking at questions and tasks from the point of view of students asking, "What problem do I need to solve?" I then gave an overview of the various assessment methods that are available and explained why I was selecting several of them to explore in detail. The main part of the book then dove deeply into ways to write multiple-choice questions, open-ended questions, and performance assessment tasks that tap higher-order thinking, based on some general principles.

The first step in assessing higher-order thinking is the same as the first step in assessing anything. You should be able to state exactly what content knowledge and skills, including thinking skills, you want to assess. The second step is to design questions or tasks that tap exactly that, knowing that any one question or task is just a sample of all the things you could have asked. Nevertheless, that question or task should require students to think at the intended level about the intended content and not require other, extraneous knowledge or skills. This book has been mainly about this second step.

Finally, to assess higher-order thinking, the criteria you use—whether in rubrics or other scoring schemes—must look for evidence of higher-order thinking as well as content knowledge. Be careful to keep the criteria open enough to accommodate divergent answers. The more open a question or performance assessment task, the more different ways there are for students to produce high-quality responses, performances, or products. Focus the criteria on the quality of the thinking and not on a list of attributes of any particular answer.

I have tried to show how giving students something to think *about* greatly assists with writing higher-order thinking questions and tasks. Typically, that takes the form of introductory material before questions or letting students use appropriate resources as they perform tasks. I have also tried to show that higher-order thinking can and should be assessed in all content areas, for students of all ages, and at a variety of difficulty levels. The method I used to do that was to work through many different examples so that you can see what assessment of higher-order thinking looks like in these divergent contexts.

I hope the "deep dive" into writing questions has been fun and has sharpened your skills. Before I end the book, I want to remind you where these questions and tasks fit in the larger picture of your teaching work.

Managing Instructional Planning

Designing and writing questions and tasks that tap higher-order thinking should fit into your curriculum and instructional planning. Plan your questions and tasks as part of this larger work. As you do, consider the following ways that the questions and tasks you design to assess higher-order thinking need to be connected to the rest of your planning, instruction, and assessment.

Although I hope this would go without saying, here's an important first principle: the criterion that you should be teaching and assessing is the standard or intended learning goal. Having said that, however, note that higher-order thinking holds an important place in most standards. Chapter 1 showed how higher-order thinking features prominently in the Common Core State Standards for English Language Arts & Literacy and Mathematics; the Next Generation Science Standards; and the College, Career, and Civic Life Framework for Social Studies State Standards. Many other state standards and most school curriculum documents also feature higher-order thinking. The issue is to place assessment of higher-order thinking where it belongs in your curriculum. In many cases, this will mean giving higher-order thinking a larger place.

The next issue follows from the first. If you are teaching higher-order thinking as part of your regular instruction, you will need strategies for sharing daily lesson learning targets that include higher-order thinking. Students should be aware that they are trying to learn certain thinking skills, and they should have "look-fors" (Moss & Brookhart, 2012) so they know what sound thinking looks like. Because questions and tasks that require higher-order thinking will result in student responses, performances, or products that are not all alike, you need an array of examples and not just one.

Similarly, if you are teaching students to use higher-order thinking, you will need instructional activities that embody these learning targets; performances of understanding (Moss & Brookhart, 2012) that can carry both instruction and formative assessment; and, ultimately, questions or tasks for summative assessment. In other words, you will be using the skills you learned in this book about writing questions and tasks that assess higher-order thinking over and over as you teach a unit. Students will use those questions and tasks to learn, to get formative feedback, and finally for a grade. Just writing one higher-order thinking question or performance assessment task, no matter how good, will not give students what they need to learn and develop higher-order thinking skills. Students need instruction and practice to learn these skills, just as they need instruction and practice to learn anything.

I have tried to emphasize all along that performance assessment tasks require appropriate rubrics in order to be complete. It's worth restating that fact in this list of management considerations. A high-quality question or task that elicits the intended content and thinking skills is one-half of the assessment; rubrics (or a rating scale, checklist, or scoring/feedback guide of some sort) are the other half. I did not cover writing rubrics in this book because my purpose here has been to discuss how to write the tasks. However, appropriate rubrics are critical, and several good books can help you do that (see, for example, Arter & Chappuis, 2006; Brookhart, 2013b).

Another issue that will arise when you use questions and tasks that elicit higher-order thinking is the issue of giving appropriate feedback. These questions and tasks help make student thinking visible. When you and your students can see what they were thinking—by listening to answers to questions or observing their responses to tasks—then the thinking itself becomes amenable to feedback. Give feedback on the quality of student thinking, not just correctness of content. What you choose to comment on sends students a message about what you think is important. You can really derail an episode of higher-order thinking if you ignore students' work in that regard. This is a big point, and it's important here because you will want to think ahead of time about the criteria for the feedback you will give and even how you might word your feedback to be helpful to students.

Resources that help teachers design tasks to assess higher-order thinking are available on the Internet, especially now that educators are interested in the Common Core and its focus on higher-order thinking. For example, in mathematics, the "Moving to the Common Core" website (www.movingtocommoncore.com/performance-tasks---mathematics.html) provides links to task-development resources, including some from the National Council of Teachers of Mathematics. In English language arts, I have already referred to Appendix B of the Common Core State Standards. In addition, an Internet search will yield a myriad of websites with examples of writing prompts. After reading this book, you should have the critical thinking skills you need to evaluate the quality of any resources you find on the Internet or in textbooks or other curricular materials.

Managing Resources and Student Behavior

If you build an organization and management infrastructure into task directions and classroom procedures, students can spend more time thinking and less time finding their crayons. Classroom routines and organization patterns are just as important for supporting assessment of higher-order thinking as for any other instruction and assessment. You want students focused on the problem solving inherent in your question or task, not on the logistics.

Performance tasks that need equipment and supplies beyond paper and pencil require strategies for distributing and collecting materials, keeping the room and desks neat, respecting equipment and using it properly, and so on. Good classroom management moves and routines will help with these logistics. Long-term projects require student planning, resources, formative checks along the way to help students stay on track and answer their questions, and often library or computer time. Good classroom management routines, especially about the use of time, will help with this. In addition, the suggestions in Chapter 6 for using a multistep design for performance assessment tasks will be helpful here. Finally, any task requiring group work needs norms, roles, and behavioral expectations as well as ways to share resources. These, too, are part of good classroom management moves and routines.

Finally, using open-ended questions works best in a supportive classroom environment where student thinking is valued, the threat of "evaluation" ("Did I get the right answer?") is minimal, and exchanging ideas is seen as important. Some classroom rules or procedures can help. For example, students should understand that they must take turns speaking. They should know to listen to one another, not just bide time while a classmate is speaking until it's their turn in the spotlight. Students should learn to listen for ideas and not personal characteristics ("his voice sounds funny"), to respond to one another and not only to the teacher, to not hog the floor, and so on. These skills are learned the same way other skills are learned: with instruction, modeling, and feedback.

A Legacy for Students

Teaching and assessing higher-order thinking is, in my view, one of the most important things you can do. Designing and writing questions and tasks that require students to use higher-order thinking is therefore an important skill. Remember the definition of higher-order thinking with which we started:

> Higher-order thinking is the mental engagement with ideas, objects, and situations in an analogical, elaborative, inductive, deductive, and otherwise transformational manner that is indicative of an orientation toward knowing as a complex, effortful, generative, evidence-seeking, and reflective enterprise. (Alexander et al., 2011, p. 53)

This is the legacy we want to leave our students. We want them to engage with knowledge, with one another, and with the world in a transformational way. Recalling information will not propel students into the future. With your help, and with your open questions and performance tasks, students can develop the kind of effortful, generative, evidence-seeking, reflective stance that will move them forward in learning and in life.

APPENDIX A

Using a Test Blueprint to Plan a Test

A test blueprint is a plan, often in chart form but sometimes also in the form of a list, that indicates the balance of content knowledge and thinking skills in a whole test. A blueprint allows you to check that your assessment aligns with the learning outcomes you intend to assess. You do this by checking that the balance among aspects of content and among levels of thinking reflects the emphasis specified in your learning outcome or outcomes. Sometimes the blueprint is called by other names: table of specifications, test plan.

I confess that I wasn't aware of what test blueprints could do when I was teaching 7th grade English. Most of my students were still learning to read, using high-interest, low-vocabulary readers designed to present one story a week. With the hindsight I acquired later, I realize that 75 percent of the questions on my weekly reading tests were about new vocabulary (at the Remember level of cognition on the revised Bloom's taxonomy) and 25 percent were about comprehending the story (at the Understand level). That is not at all what I intended; it just never occurred to me to evaluate the set of questions on the reading test as a whole. It's too late for me to go back and provide more accurate assessment for those 7th graders. It's not too late for you and your current and future students.

Figure A.1 shows an example of a simple blueprint that would have produced a much better test than the one I created. The reading test sketched out in this blueprint has a better balance of content and includes higher-order thinking, which my reading tests did not.

Figure A.1 A Blueprint for a Reading Test with Points in Three Cognitive Levels

Learning Objectives	Remember	Understand	Analyze	Total
Define new vocabulary words	5			5 (17%)
Use new vocabulary words in sentences		5		5 (17%)
Comprehend the main points in the story		10		10 (33%)
Connect elements from the story (character, plot, or setting) with own life or other texts			10	10 (33%)
Total	5 (17%)	15 (50%)	10 (33%)	30 (100%)

The first column lists the major learning objectives the assessment will cover. The outline can be as simple or as detailed as you need to describe the content domain for your learning goals. The column headings across the top list some of the classifications in the cognitive domain of the revised Bloom's taxonomy. You could use any other taxonomy of thinking as well. Notice I have used only three of Bloom's cognitive levels: Remember, Understand, and Analyze. I could also have included all six levels and simply had blank columns under Apply, Evaluate, and Create.

The cells in the blueprint show the number of points allocated for each learning objective at particular levels of thinking. You can also include more specific learning objectives within the cells (for example, the cell "Comprehend the main points in the story/Understand" could contain, for a particular story, "Retells the plot accurately" or "Describes how the plot and characters communicate the theme of loneliness"). The number of points you select for each cell should reflect the balance of content and thinking skills from your learning outcomes and your instruction.

Making a blueprint allows you to fully describe the composition and emphasis of the assessment as a whole, so you can interpret it accurately. In the example shown in Figure A.1, I could say my reading test score represented equal amounts of knowing and using new vocabulary, comprehending the story, and making connections from other texts to the story.

Blueprints are also handy for identifying places where you need to make adjustments. For example, if I had made a chart or list for my original reading test and seen that knowing and using vocabulary words accounted for 75 percent of the points and comprehension accounted for 25 percent, I would have known I needed to adjust. Adjusting the balance of your assessment questions is much easier to do before you write the questions. At the planning stage, it's just a matter of moving points around. After you have written a test, revision requires rewriting.

Every cell need not be filled. Fill only the cells that reflect your learning goals. And the points in each cell do not all need to be represented by 1-point (e.g., multiple-choice) test items. For example, the 10 points in the cell for connecting elements from the story with other texts or one's own life could be one 10-point essay, two 5-point essays, or any combination that totaled 10 points.

Blueprints make the task of writing questions for a test easier. The blueprint tells you exactly what kinds of questions you need, and how many. Blueprints sometimes help you plan additional assessments that are a better fit with your learning outcomes. For example, I might have decided, upon looking at this reading test blueprint, to remove the "connecting texts" from the test and assign a brief in-class essay instead. That would have left me with a shorter, simpler test and an essay assignment, which I could then combine for a final grade for this section of the reading unit.

APPENDIX B

Using a Protocol to Review Assessment Tasks

A protocol is a structure for professional discussion. It serves as a mechanism for colleagues to give and receive feedback on all kinds of professional decisions, practices, and policies. The protocol in this appendix is useful for reviewing teacher assignments, and as applied to this book that means reviewing performance assessment tasks. I have used this protocol in professional development for reviewing assignments to determine the ways in which they assessed higher-order thinking. After one such session, a participant said, "We needed to do this!" Close analysis of an assignment can only happen with the help of the questions in each of the protocol's steps. As Easton (2009) says, protocols "serve as a kind of co-facilitator" (p. 1) for professional discussions.

Use the Standards in Practice Protocol to focus on the quality of a performance task and its fitness for assessing the knowledge and skills, including higher-order thinking skills, you intended to assess. If you use the protocol before you administer the performance assessment, you can use the results to revise the assessment and also to inform the instructional planning you will do to ready your students for the assessment. If you use the protocol after administering the performance assessment, you can use it to score student work (optional Step 9) and to evaluate how well the work fulfills intentions for assessing a particular standard(s) or learning outcome(s).

This protocol originated with the Education Trust. Easton (2009) modified it and included an assessment of the rigor of the assignment. I have modified it further, adding or modifying questions about cognitive level, task structure, and difficulty in order to match the framework for creating tasks presented in this book.

Standards in Practice Protocol

Overview: This protocol can be used to assess assignments, assessment prompts, and instructional tasks. Presenters present and explain an assignment, an assessment, or a task. Then participants discuss the task according to the protocol; this discussion serves as feedback to the presenter. The presenter reflects, and the group debriefs.

Number of Participants: 6 to 8, plus facilitator and presenter

Steps (times based on a 60-minute session)

Step 1: Choosing the Assignment (preparation for session)

Step 2: Presenting the Assignment (5 minutes)

- The presenter can present as much context for the assignment as she wants, but the assignment should stand on its own for examination.
- The presenter may also want to explain how the assignment fits within the context of a unit and of the class.

Step 3: Trying the Assignment (5 minutes, more if time allows)

- Presenter steps outside the process at this point, taking notes but not participating.
- Participants try the assignment themselves, if possible with the time, space, and materials provided; if not, they should "rehearse" the assignment by imagining the steps students would take.

Step 4: Analyzing the Assignment (10 minutes)

- Participants brainstorm what the assignment requires of students. They might assess the following characteristics, known collectively as KASAB (Killion, 2007):

» Knowledge (what students need to know)
» Attitude (how students should feel about the assignment to be successful)
» Skills (what students need to be able to do)
» Aspiration (what students believe they can do in terms of the assignment)
» Behavior (what students actually do to complete the assignment)

Step 5: Determining the Cognitive Level of the Assignment (5 minutes)

• Participants discuss the levels of the revised Bloom's taxonomy (Remember, Understand, Apply, Analyze, Evaluate, Create) that apply to the assignment. Other cognitive taxonomies (e.g., Webb, SOLO) may be used instead.

Step 6: Assessing the Assignment's Task Structure (5 minutes)

• Participants judge the level of structure provided in the assignment for the target group of students and determine if the assignment is appropriately open/closed. The following indicators may be used to complete this step:

» What amount of structure is provided for defining the problem or conceptualizing the question on which the task is based?
» What amount of structure is provided for the strategies and materials students will use to do the assignment?
» What amount of structure is provided for acceptable solutions and preparation of the final product or performance?

Step 7: Assessing the Assignment's Difficulty (5 minutes)

• Participants judge the difficulty of the assignment for the target group of students and determine if the assignment is at an appropriate level of difficulty. The following indicators may be used to complete this step:

» What is the difficulty level of the directions for the assignment?
» What is the difficulty level of the task itself (i.e., the inquiry or construction the students are being asked to do)?
» What is the difficulty level of the materials students will use to complete the assignment (i.e., things they must read, view, and interpret)?
» Are these difficulty levels appropriate for the target group of students? Can/should the materials or other aspects of the task be tiered to accommodate different difficulty levels?

Step 8: Developing Scoring Criteria (5 minutes)

- Participants develop a list of criteria that they might use to score student work resulting from the given assignment.
- They do not develop a complete rubric (with descriptions for each scoring level for each criterion), only the criteria for a rubric.
- If the assignment has not yet been given, the criteria can be used to develop a rubric before giving the assignment.

Step 9: Scoring Student Work (5 minutes; step applies only if student work is provided)

- If student work is available, participants apply the scoring criteria from Step 8 (if the students were given a rubric, participants apply the rubric) to the work, determining how well the work fulfills the criteria as well as how well the criteria describe the actual work.

Step 10: Discussing Revision of the Assignment (5 minutes)

- Based on their work in the previous steps, participants determine how they might improve the assessment (assignment, activity), acting upon a belief that student work is influenced by the quality of the assignment.
- Participants might also discuss the appropriate instruction that would lead up to the assignment as well as the conditions under which students might best work through the assessment.

Step 11: Presenter Reflection (5 minutes)

- The presenter, who has been taking notes during this process, reflects aloud about what the participants have accomplished.

Step 12: Debriefing (5 minutes)

- The presenter and the participants, led by the facilitator, discuss how well the process worked.

Source: From *Protocols for Professional Learning* (pp. 54–56), by L. B. Easton, Alexandria, VA: ASCD. Copyright 2009 by ASCD.

References

Abrami, P. C., Bernard, R. M., Borokhovski, E., Wade, A., Surkes, M. A., Tamim, R., & Zhang, D. (2008, December). Instructional interventions affecting critical thinking skills and dispositions: A stage 1 meta-analysis. *Review of Educational Research, 78*(4), 1102–1134.

Alexander, P. A., Dinsmore, D. L., Fox, E., Grossnickle, E. M., Loughlin, S. M., Maggioni, L., Parkinson, M. M., & Winters, F. I. (2011). Higher-order thinking and knowledge: Domain-general and domain-specific trends and future directions. In G. Schraw & D. R. Robinson (Eds.), *Assessment of higher order thinking skills* (pp. 47–88). Charlotte, NC: Information Age Publishing.

Anderson, L. W., & Krathwohl, D. R. (Eds.). (2001). *A taxonomy for learning, teaching, and assessing: A revision of Bloom's taxonomy of educational objectives* (Complete ed.). New York: Longman.

Arter, J. A., & Chappuis, J. (2006). *Creating and recognizing quality rubrics*. Boston: Pearson.

Bennett, R. E. (1993). On the meanings of constructed response. In R. E. Bennett & W. C. Ward (Eds.), *Construction versus choice in cognitive measurement* (pp. 1–27). Hillsdale, NJ: Lawrence Erlbaum.

Biggs, J. B., & Collis, K. F. (1982). *Evaluating the quality of learning: The SOLO taxonomy*. New York: Academic Press.

Bloom, B. S., Engelhart, M. D., Furst, E. J., Hill, W. H., & Krathwohl, D. R. (1956). *Taxonomy of educational objectives, Handbook I: Cognitive domain*. Reading, MA: Addison Wesley.

Bloomfield, A., Wayland, S. C., Rhoades, E., Blodgett, A., Linck, J., & Ross, S. (2010). *What makes listening difficult? Factors affecting second language listening comprehension*. College Park, MD: University of Maryland Center for Advanced Study of Language.

Bransford, J. D., & Stein, B. S. (1984). *The IDEAL problem solver*. New York: W. H. Freeman.

Brookhart, S. M. (1999). *The art and science of classroom assessment: The missing part of pedagogy.* (ASHE-ERIC Higher Education Report, *27*[1]). Washington, DC: George Washington University, Graduate School of Education and Human Development.

Brookhart, S. M. (2008). *How to give effective feedback to your students.* Alexandria, VA: ASCD.

Brookhart, S. M. (2010). *How to assess higher-order thinking skills in your classroom.* Alexandria, VA: ASCD.

Brookhart, S. M. (2013a). *Grading and group work: How do I assess individual learning when students work together?* Alexandria, VA: ASCD.

Brookhart, S. M. (2013b). *How to create and use rubrics for formative assessment and grading.* Alexandria, VA: ASCD.

Brookhart, S. M. (2013c). The public understanding of assessment in educational reform in the United States. *Oxford Review of Education, 39*(1), 52–71.

Brookhart, S. M., & Nitko, A. J. (2015). *Educational assessment of students* (7th ed.). Boston: Pearson.

Brown, G., & Wragg, E. (1993). *Questioning.* London: Routledge.

BSCS. (2005). *Doing science: The process of scientific inquiry.* Colorado Springs, CO: BSCS Center for Curriculum Development. NIH Publication No. 05-5564.

Buck, L. B., Bretz, S. L., & Towns, M. H. (2008, September). Characterizing the level of inquiry in the undergraduate laboratory. *Journal of College Science Teaching, 38*(1), 52–58.

Dodge, B. (2002). *WebQuest taskonomy: A taxonomy of tasks.* Retrieved from http://webquest.sdsu.edu/taskonomy.html

Dr. Seuss. (1957). *The cat in the hat.* New York: Random House.

Easton, L. B. (2009). *Protocols for professional learning.* Alexandria, VA: ASCD.

Fay, M. E., Grove, N. P., Towns, M. H., & Bretz, S. L. (2007). A rubric to characterize inquiry in the undergraduate chemistry laboratory. *Chemistry Education Research and Practice, 8*(2), 212–219.

Higgins, S., Hall, E., Baumfield, V., & Moseley, D. (2005). A meta-analysis of the impact of the implementation of thinking skills approaches on pupils. In *Research Evidence in Education Library.* London: EPPI-Centre, Social Science Research Unit, Institute of Education, University of London.

Kansas State Board of Education. (2013, April 16). *Kansas standards for history, government, and social studies.* Topeka, KS: Author. Available: www.ksde.org.

Killion, J. (2007). *Assessing impact: Evaluating staff development* (2nd ed.). Thousand Oaks, CA: Corwin.

Koedinger, K. (2010). *Cognitive task analysis: Think alouds and difficulty factors assessment.* Presentation, Pittsburgh Science of Learning Center.

Michaels, S., Shouse, A. W., & Schweingruber, H. A. (2007). *Ready, set, science! Putting research to work in K–8 science classrooms.* Washington, DC: National Academies Press.

Moss, C. M., & Brookhart, S. M. (2009). *Advancing formative assessment in every classroom: A guide for instructional leaders.* Alexandria, VA: ASCD.

Moss, C. M., & Brookhart, S. M. (2012). *Learning targets: Helping students aim for understanding in today's lesson.* Alexandria, VA: ASCD.

National Council for the Social Studies (NCSS). (2013). *The college, career, and civic life (C3) framework for social studies state standards: Guidance for enhancing the rigor of K–12 civics, economics, geography, and history.* Silver Spring, MD: Author. Available: www.socialstudies.org/c3

National Governors Association Center for Best Practices (NGA Center) & Council of Chief State School Officers (CCSSO). (2010a). *Common Core State Standards for English language arts & literacy in history/social studies, science, and technical subjects.* Washington, DC: Author.

NGA Center & CCSSO. (2010b). *Common Core State Standards for mathematics.* Washington, DC: Author.

National Research Council. (2012). *A framework for K–12 science education: Practices, crosscutting concepts, and core ideas.* Committee on a Conceptual Framework for New K–12 Science Education Standards. Washington, DC: National Academies Press.

Olson, S., & Loucks-Horsley, S. (Eds.). (2000). *Inquiry and the National Science Education Standards: A guide for teaching and learning.* Washington, DC: National Academies Press.

Pajares, F. (2006). Self-efficacy during childhood and adolescence: Implications for teachers and parents. In F. Pajares & T. Urdan (Eds.), *Self-efficacy beliefs of adolescents* (pp. 339–367). Greenwich, CT: Information Age Publishing.

Pogrow, S. (2005). HOTS revisited: A thinking development approach to reducing the learning gap after grade 3. *Phi Delta Kappan, 87*(1), 64–75.

Schommer, M., Calvert, C., Gariglietti, G., & Bajaj, A. (1997). The development of epistemological beliefs among secondary students: A longitudinal study. *Journal of Educational Psychology, 89*(1), 37–40.

Small, M. (2012). *Good questions: Great ways to differentiate mathematics instruction* (2nd ed.). New York: Teachers College Press.

Snow, R. E. (1993). Construct validity and constructed-response tests. In R. E. Bennett & W. C. Ward (Eds.), *Construction versus choice in cognitive measurement* (pp. 45–60). Hillsdale, NJ: Lawrence Erlbaum.

Stiggins, R. J. (1992). High quality classroom assessment: What does it really mean? *Educational Measurement: Issues and Practice, 11*(2), 35–39.

Stiggins, R. J., & Chappuis, J. (2011). *An introduction to student-involved assessment for learning* (6th ed.). Boston: Pearson.

Webb, N. L. (2002). *Alignment study in language arts, mathematics, science, and social studies of state standards and assessments for four states.* Washington, DC: Council of Chief State School Officers.

Index

Note: Page numbers followed by an italicized *f* indicate information contained in figures.

About the Author

Susan M. Brookhart, PhD, is an independent educational consultant based in Helena, Montana. She has taught both elementary and middle school. She was professor and chair of the Department of Educational Foundations and Leadership at Duquesne University, where she currently serves as senior research associate in the Center for Advancing the Study of Teaching and Learning in the School of Education. She has been the education columnist for *National Forum,* the journal of Phi Kappa Phi, and editor of *Educational Measurement: Issues and Practice,* a journal of the National Council on Measurement in Education. She is the author or coauthor of several books, including ASCD's *How to Give Effective Feedback to Your Students, How to Assess Higher-Order Thinking Skills in Your Classroom, How to Create and Use Rubrics for Formative Assessment and Grading, Advancing Formative Assessment in Every Classroom, Learning Targets: Helping Students Aim for Understanding in Today's Lesson,* and *Grading and Group Work.* She may be reached at susanbrookhart@bresnan.net.

Related ASCD Resources: Assessment and Thinking Skills

At the time of publication, the following ASCD resources were available (ASCD stock numbers appear in parentheses). For up-to-date information about ASCD resources, go to www.ascd.org. You can search the complete archives of *Educational Leadership* at http://www.ascd.org/el.

Professional Interest Communities

Visit the ASCD website and scroll to the bottom to click on "professional interest communities." Within these communities, find information about professional educators who have formed groups around topics like "Assessment for Learning."

ASCD EDge Groups

Exchange ideas and connect with other educators interested in various topics, including Assessment for Learning, Assessment and Grading, Effective Feedback, and Formative Assessment on the social networking site ASCD EDge™.

PD Online

Assessment: Designing Performance Assessments, 2nd Ed. (#PD11OC108)

Formative Assessment and the Common Core Standards: English Language Arts/Literacy (#PD13OC005M)

Formative Assessment and the Common Core Standards: Mathematics (#PD13OC006)

These and other online courses are available at www.ascd.org/pdonline

Print Products

Checking for Understanding: Formative Assessment Techniques for Your Classroom by Douglas Fisher and Nancy Frey (#107023)

The Formative Assessment Action Plan: Practical Steps to More Successful Teaching and Learning by Nancy Frey and Douglas Fisher (#111013)

Formative Assessment Strategies for Every Classroom: An ASCD Action Tool, 2nd Edition by Susan M. Brookhart (#111005)

Grading Smarter, Not Harder: Assessment Strategies That Motivate Kids and Help Them Learn by Myron Dueck (#114003)

Great Performances: Creating Classroom-Based Assessment Tasks, 2nd Edition by Larry Lewin and Betty Jean Shoemaker (#110038)

How to Assess Higher-Order Thinking Skills in Your Classroom by Susan M. Brookhart (#109111)

How to Create and Use Rubrics for Formative Assessment and Grading by Susan M. Brookhart (#112001)

Transformative Assessment by W. James Popham (#108018)

DVDs

Assessment for 21st Century Learning DVD Set (#610010)

Formative Assessment in Content Areas DVD Series (#609034)

Learning to Think... Thinking to Learn: The Pathway to Achievement (#607087)

The Power of Formative Assessment to Advance Learning 3 DVD Set (#608066)

The Whole Child Initiative

THE WHOLE CHILD The Whole Child Initiative helps schools and communities create learning environments that allow students to be healthy, safe, engaged, supported, and challenged. To learn more about other books and resources that relate to the whole child, visit www.wholechildeducation.org.

For more information: send e-mail to member@ascd.org; call 1-800-933-2723 or 703-578-9600, press 2; send a fax to 703-575-5400; or write to Information Services, ASCD, 1703 N. Beauregard St., Alexandria, VA 22311-1714 USA.